EVERYDAY MODIFICATIONS FOR YOUR TRIUMPH SPITFIRE, HERALD, VITESSE AND GT6

How to Make Your Classic Car Easier to Live With and Enjoy

EVERYDAY MODIFICATIONS FOR YOUR TRIUMPH SPITFIRE, HERALD, VITESSE AND GT6

How to Make Your Classic Car Easier to Live With and Enjoy

Iain Ayre

THE CROWOOD PRESS

First published in 2016 by
The Crowood Press Ltd
Ramsbury, Marlborough
Wiltshire SN8 2HR

www.crowood.com

British Library Cataloguing-in-Publication Data
A catalogue record for this book is available from the British Library.

ISBN 978 1 78500 175 8

Typeset by Servis Filmsetting Ltd, Stockport, Cheshire

Printed and bound in Malaysia by Times Offset (M) Sdn Bhd

contents

introduction

'Straight from the horse's mouth' is an excellent adage suggesting where you would find good advice, and in this book it is fulfilled on three counts: this is because here we have an author who owned a good few Triumphs back when they were still fairly current; a technical consultant who has run a Triumph restoration business for decades; and input from a designer who worked at one of the prime developers of tuning accessories for Triumphs.

Iain Ayre has been driving and writing books and articles about Triumphs, MGs, Jaguars, TVRs and other British classics for longer than he cares to remember: hence the scarf made of event lanyards.

Randy Zoller has been racing, restoring and repairing Triumphs, Healeys, Morgans, TVRs and other British classics for longer than he cares to remember as well. Check him out at www.britishheritagemotorsports. com.

Iain's default/favourite motor car during the 1970s was the Triumph Vitesse, alternating between convertible and saloon versions. This was one of the better examples.

Many of the Triumphs photographed for this book are left-hand drive. This is because I live in the Pacific Northwest, which was a significant export market for Triumph and MG. Much of the research for the book also took place at a Triumph restoration shop, in San Diego, California. Something like half of all Spitfire production went to North America, and many of them are still there. On the Vancouver Craigslist, a free advertising site, on a random day in June 2015, there were twenty-nine Triumphs for sale.

My Triumphs have comprised an early Herald convertible with a cardboard dash; a Herald estate with crumbling outriggers on which a rear trailing arm came adrift under way, which was even more of a surprise than a previous swing-arm-related rear-wheel jack-up; a Vitesse Six convertible, and a couple of Vitesse saloons; two Spitfires that were bought at December prices, driven through the winter at college to save money, then painted and sold in June to fund long holidays in France; a late-model GT6; and finally a Midge, which is a 1930s-style kit car intended for a Herald or a square-tube replacement Herald chassis, and which in my case was the first 6-cylinder example. This was based on my mother's crumbling Vitesse, which she crashed, and which was transformed into a Midge and given back to her: she drove it with style and panache until her eighties.

I have nearly killed myself swerving in a Herald convertible with swing axles; I have enjoyed the relative comfort of sitting on the front tyre of a Vitesse in weekend sunshine while working on its engine, in marked contrast with the back pain or grovelling involved in fixing lesser cars; and I have match-ported and polished six intake tracts while sorting out some hardened valve seats for the Midge. In recent years I have enjoyed writing regularly for *Triumph World* magazine, which is an excellent Triumph resource with a knowledgeable and hands-on Triumph-owning editor, has intriguing and inspiring stories, and a set of very useful advertisements that tell you exactly where all the key Triumph spares are to be found.

Triumphs have been fun to own, and I recommend them.

FOCUS

This book is concerned with improving the 4-cylinder Spitfire and Herald, and the 6-cylinder Vitesse and GT6, with engines ranging in size from 948cc to 1998cc. The larger Triumph engines found in the TR6 and the Triumph 2500 were not fitted to the smaller Triumphs, and used more substantial gearboxes and differentials. The drivetrains fitted to the smaller Triumphs were marginal when fitted to 2-litre engines, and would not survive long behind a 2500cc engine. However, the book does include information on the engines and gearboxes out of the TR6, which can be used in the smaller Triumphs to great effect.

Randy Zoller has run the British Heritage Motorsports (.com) restoration and vintage-racing workshop in San Diego for decades: he is an automotive archaeologist as well as a musician and a master mechanic.

Triumphs remain among the world's favourite reasonable-budget classics, not least because of spares availability and their robust chassis as well as their general charm and good looks.

HISTORY AND BACKGROUND

The Triumph story starts in 1886 with bicycles, and then motorcycles in 1902. The first cars appeared in 1923 in the form of the 10/20, built to a design by Lea-Francis. The Super 7 was next, selling well from 1927 to 1934, but rather than competing for the mass market with Austin and Ford, Triumph changed direction towards making expensive cars such as the Southern Cross and the Gloria, and created just three straight-8-engined Dolomites, inspired by the Alfa Romeo 8C. The 1930s were hard times, and Triumph ran into financial trouble, first selling the motorcycle division, and then going into liquidation in 1939. The company was bought out of bankruptcy and revived, but the factory was flattened during the war.

The Standard Motor Company's flamboyant Captain John Black then fell out with William Lyons, and bought what little was left of Triumph, mostly the name, with the idea of building a more prestigious brand than Standard to compete against what was then SS, which became SS Jaguar, and then just Jaguar when the letters SS acquired unfortunate Nazi connotations.

The Standard Motor Company had started up in 1903 in Coventry, and after rather less of a bucking-bronco ride through the 1920s than Triumph, settled down in the 1930s to producing a respectable number of Standard 9s and 10s, worthy but dull low-to-medium-budget family cars.

The 1948 Vanguard was the first properly post-war British car design, and was very American in its styling,

The Triumph name goes back a long way. This 1950 Renown in aluminium resembled the post-war Bentleys, giving an indication of the target audience.

The early 1950s Mayflower rather misfired: it was an expensive upmarket small car, a new concept that hadn't really previously existed, and it went a bit wild on the 'Razor-Edge' styling. Like Marmite, it was either loved or loathed.

although it was really too stubby to look as good as its contemporary period American designs, which have the physical length to resolve those dramatic lines properly. Standard continued to develop along the same lines, with mostly budget cars; in 1953 they offered the cheapest four-door car in Britain. And also in the same year the Triumph name came back to life with the TR2.

The Standard name was now associated with cheapness, but the Triumph name still carried a premium, so the Standard name was eased out and dropped. We can see the same thing happening now with BMW: their name and brand is losing its status with the financially successful mass sales of a quarter-million units annually, and people will eventually realize that when everyone has a BMW, it's no longer a premium product. The company is therefore now in the Ford Cortina/Sierra market, and other higher-class brand names will be bought in to replace the BMW

brand – and one of the names BMW has bought for this marketing process is Triumph.

THE HERALD ERA

The Herald story starts in 1959 when Standard was selling the Standard 8 and 10, powered by an 803cc and 948cc 4-cylinder engine, respectively. The internal name for the upcoming Herald project was Zobo, but Standard Triumph's flag-related naming theme was retained with the more upmarket Triumph brand name, and thus the Herald was christened. The name also referred to managing director Alec Dick's boat.

Small Standards tended to be dumpy and dull, but at least had a modern monocoque: the Herald retreated to an old-fashioned separate chassis that was used for all its descendants and derivatives, although the body design

The Herald remains an excellent starter classic, available in fine condition for a few thousand pounds, and in rescuable condition for a few hundred. Pretty coachwork, four seats, cheap repairs, 40mpg (7ltr/100km) fuel economy: a bargain.

was dramatically modern, the work of Italian Giovanni Michelotti.

The adoption of a separate chassis was not really by choice, but was the result of Standard's body supplier Fisher no longer being helpful, having been bought by competitor BMC. Sidestepping big, expensive and capital-intensive monocoque structures and breaking down the manufacture of the Herald into smaller and more manageable chunks made a good deal of sense. Tooling up for a new car with a separate chassis was theoretically both cheaper and faster, and the Mini and the Anglia were both a potential threat.

The separate chassis also allowed great flexibility in terms of the model range. Heralds and Vitesses have completely detachable and largely interchangeable body tubs, roofs and front ends, which allowed for the swift development and availability of coupé, convertible and van versions, and which is why you see the occasional Vitesse estate: these may not have existed officially, but it was easy enough to collect and assemble one.

You can also mix and match Spitfires and GT6s to some extent, and for some, the ultimate small Triumph is the GT6fire, or Spit 6 – a GT6 in which the coupé body is replaced with a convertible Spitfire tub, but retains the 6-cylinder mechanics and the power-bulged bonnet.

The separate chassis also provides excellent benefits for you and me as enthusiasts and weekend mechanics – if you have a good chassis but a bad body or vice versa, you can find more spares of each, and mix and match to achieve a solid car for a sensible price, although identity complications may arise.

The pure luxury of the huge flip front is also only possible with a separate chassis, as monocoques use the front wings as stressed members, which makes the bodywork

11

harder to repair and the engines harder to work on. Sitting on the wheel of a Herald-descendant Triumph while fixing the engine is a definite bonus – although you must *never* sit on an uninflated tyre: it can sag, and the treads then violently pinch delicate flesh like twenty mole-grips. This is a mistake you will only make once.

The origins of the Herald family's suspension are a good story. Triumph's Harry Webster was making good progress on the future Herald mechanicals, with transverse leaf springs and independent suspension planned at both ends, and rack steering. Somebody decided that matching the astonishingly tight turning circle of a London taxi would be a brilliant idea. Nobody seems to have asked if the customers were likely to want this, or even questioned whether it was a good idea, but the front axle was redesigned with double wishbones to allow the car to turn on the proverbial and contemporary sixpence. Anybody still using this facility on fifty-year-old trunnions had better keep them well oiled, though.

As it happens, the Herald family's front suspension thus ended up as notably good as its rear suspension is bad. Rear-axle jack-up on hard cornering has probably scared as many enthusiastic Triumph drivers as the careless use of London taxis' amazing turning circle has hospitalized motorcycle dispatch riders.

The origins of the body are also a good story. Michelotti had proposed to design and prototype a new body in three months on a sale-or-return basis, for which Triumph would pay nothing if they didn't like it. Webster grabbed at this, although as the three months dragged on somewhat beyond the original deadline, he had to physically drive to Italy and to Michelotti's house, stand over his shoulder and encourage him personally. The end of 1957 saw the first prototype, and it was dramatic and pretty enough to invigorate the whole company. Italians seem to be genetically unable to design anything ugly, apart from the obese SUV version of the new Fiat 500. Mass-produced British cars in 1957 tended to have the look of a plum pudding with portholes, so the sharp lines, the tailfins, the slim pillars and the elegant glasshouse of the Herald must have been genuinely exciting.

The Herald was finally launched in 1959. The Mini and Anglia were supposed to have been leapfrogged and overtaken by the theoretically speedy development offered by the separate Triumph chassis, but assorted delays meant that the Herald appeared more or less concurrently with them, rather than showing up first and stealing their thunder.

Build quality was poor, as the bitty assembly method encouraged errors to creep in, and the Herald was also relatively expensive – it was only really saved by its sharp and attractive Italian lines. The dangerous rear suspension wasn't too much of a problem, as the original 948cc engine wasn't fast enough to encourage drivers to get into trouble.

In 1960, Standard Triumph was in deep financial trouble, with the Standard-branded cars not doing well and a glut of unsold TR3As, and the company was ripe for a takeover by British Leyland, which duly took place.

The Herald was perceived to have a future, although the Standard brand models just evaporated, and the inherited Standard 948cc 34.5bhp engine was enlarged to 1147cc and 39bhp in 1961. This was a tricky process, as the cylinder block was physically small and there was no chance of any funding for a completely new engine. The extra capacity was achieved by offset-boring the cylinders, which usefully improved the efficiency and torque numbers at a very reasonable cost. Offset-boring is currently used by amateur Mini enthusiasts to enlarge 1275cc Mini engines to 1430cc, so it really does cost very little compared to developing a new engine.

The process of expanding with cheaply developed new models based on the same substructure began to unfold. The estate version of the Herald appeared in 1961, essentially just requiring the design and construction of a new tailgate, roof, floor and a folding rear seat. The Courier van followed in 1962, requiring not much more than the replacement of the rear side windows with steel panels and the deletion of some creature comforts. It was expensive for a van, and didn't sell very well.

The rare and rather pointless 948cc coupé, which really just had a less convenient steel top with no rear passenger headroom and poor rear three-quarter visibility, lived for only a few years, but its rarity now makes it desirable.

The 12/50 offered better trim and more power at 51bhp, with disc brakes and a Webasto sunroof, and the standard 1147cc engine in the standard 1200 model was improved to 48bhp.

The 13/60 refreshed the Herald range in 1967, with the engine enlarged to 1296cc and power increased to 61bhp, and with a much more modern bonnet derived from the Vitesse but featuring only two headlamps. This blended seamlessly with the rest of the body whether in convertible, saloon or estate form. The last Heralds were made in 1971.

THE VITESSE

For the Vitesse, back we go to 1962, and the Vanguard-sourced, 2-litre, straight-six engine that had been achieved by extending the 803cc casting by two cylinders was sleeved down to 1596cc and fitted to a strengthened Herald chassis with a new twin-headlamp front end. This was christened the Vitesse – French for 'speed' – after the 1934–36 Triumph Gloria Vitesse. The gearbox and differential were uprated, but not by much, and an overdrive was an option. The swing-axle rear suspension was not improved, sadly. The interior featured better seats and more woodwork, and the car sold well. Performance for a four-seater with reasonable fuel economy was pretty good, and the exhaust note from the revvy short-stroke straight-six was, and remains, delicious.

The Vitesse 2-litre followed in 1966, with 1998cc, 95bhp, 100mph (160km/h), further detail transmission improvements, fatter wheels and the same swinging rear axle. The years 1968 to 1971 saw the final iteration of the Vitesse, with 104bhp, detailed visual updates and finally an improvement to the rear axle with wishbones and Rotoflex drive couplings. The rear suspension had now been upgraded to 'not too bad'.

Above and next page top: The Vitesse is essentially a Herald with a 6-cylinder engine and some barely adequate beefing up of the running gear. The earlier 1600cc engine loves to rev, and issues pure music from its pea-shooter tailpipe.

If you're restoring and improving a Triumph, why not use a modern colour? This Spit was painted by a graphic designer, and the colour has worked very well indeed.

THE SPITFIRE

With the MG/Austin Healey Spridget already selling well, the obvious clever move for BL was to continue selling two sports cars that would compete head-to-head with each other – so that's what they did. The Spitfire was built in various forms between 1962 and 1981, paralleling and competing with the Midget from 1961 to 1980, after which the British sports-car market was presented to Mazda.

The Spitfire wasn't quite as easy a conversion for the Herald chassis as coupés or estates, but essentially the side body outriggers were replaced with shorter versions, a few inches were cut out of the centre, and the front crossbeam was changed. The car's sills became a structural member, unlike the other Herald-based saloons.

The engine was a modified 1200, with an extra carb and 63bhp, and the very good Herald steering and front suspension were retained as well as the dodgy rear suspension, which was less forgivable on a sports car than on a saloon.

Above and next page: The Spitfire remains ubiquitous and easily and cheaply available, and is still as much fun to drive as it was in 1962. Again, the separate chassis makes it very repairable, and parts are cheap and plentiful.

The Triumph was upmarket from the MG, with wind-up windows and an optional steel hardtop, and before long, wood veneers appeared in the cockpit. The Mk II of 1965 offered 67bhp, better seats, carpets rather than mats, and a very useful 38mpg (7.4ltr/100km). The Mk III of 1967 had a quite different look, with the raised 'bone in teeth' bumpers that were required for US sales. Some prefer the earlier look, but a lot of people like the higher bumper just as well. The Mk III also featured what has turned out to be the enthusiasts' favourite Spitfire engine, the 1296cc with 75bhp.

In 1970 the Mk IV experienced the downhill slide of power numbers as emissions regulations strangled performance, but there was a successful modernization of the rear end with a Karmann-styled chopped-off tail, bearing a strong design connection to Karmann's transformation of the TR4 into the TR6. The car's styling was definitely not ruined, and both early and later Spitfires look good. The visible welded front-wing seams with

their trim also disappeared and gave way to smooth, more modern wing tops, and the interior was given several upgrades including the relocation of the clocks in front of the driver, which makes more sense even though it requires different RHD and LHD dashboards and wiring looms. Importantly, the rear suspension was improved in the Mk IV of November 1970, with more negative camber and a wider track, and there was a sharply styled factory hardtop available that looked very nice indeed. The Mk IV is many people's favourite Spit.

The Spitfire 1500 of 1974 received a 1493cc engine shared with the MG Midget. It only had 53bhp, powering a car that now weighed 1,900lb (860kg) as compared to the Spitfire's original 1,600lb (725kg), but it did provide some useful torque. Some would say it's not really a sports-car engine, and it is true that it doesn't like to rev. It would be safe to say that if you like charging about a bit, you'd probably enjoy the 1300, and if you like touring and cruising, the 1500 would be more likely to suit you.

THE GT6

The 1966 GT6 started off as the GT4, a proposed fast-back version of the Spitfire. Designed again by Giovanni Michelotti, it was very pretty, but the added weight of the long steel roof and glasshouse made the performance with the 1147cc engine too pathetic, so it was shelved until the aerodynamics of the fastback proved successful in racing and reinvigorated interest in the concept. At this point the 6-cylinder engine shared with the Vitesse was fitted, and thus the GT6 was born in 1966. The engine wouldn't fit under the Spitfire bonnet, hence the charismatic power bulge. It must be one of very few genuine automotive power bulges, as it is not just cosmetic: the Spitfire bonnet won't clear the rocker cover of the straight six. The GT6 was fast, which made rear suspension development urgent, and in 1968 lower wishbones were added, which helped to sort it out. The GT6 Mk III in 1970 shared the Rotoflex couplings and geometry improvements of the Mk IV Spitfire, and charged on until 1973.

The extra bodyweight and tailgate that had required the fitting of the bigger engine was at the back, and balanced the additional forward weight of the extra cast-iron cylinders of the six, so the handling of the GT6 is not bad at all. My own 1972 example was regularly given some proper exercise, and overall it behaved well when pushed, apart from blowing a head gasket.

SPECIALS AND KIT CARS

The combination of box sections, rudimentary if any rust-proofing, acid rain, road salt and a long history have meant that Triumph Heralds and their derivatives have crumbled enthusiastically. However, the main chassis lasts longer than the bodywork and was used under many kit cars, which remain available for very reasonable prices. The most numerous are Burlington, Moss, Spartan and Midge. The Midge remains available from the Midge Owners' and Builders' Club and is built from plans in plywood, so if you end up with a Triumph body that's beyond repair but still has a good chassis and mechanicals, you can reclaim it as a 1930s-style open sports car. It's fun to drive these, not least because they delight the general public and cost very little.

Above and next page: The GT6 is a Spitfire with a straight six and a very pretty coupé body. The extra weight balances the heavy engine very nicely, making an overdrive-equipped GT6 an excellent sports tourer.

BEYOND EVERYDAY MODIFICATIONS

If you are enthused by this book or simply by the prospect of owning and improving a nice little sports car, and find you enjoy the process of making a small Triumph go faster and handle better, you might want to go further.

The stories I write for *Triumph World* magazine tend to focus on the unusual, because there are already plenty of easily available and beautifully restored cars within easy reach of its editor.

The case studies chapter at the end of the book features a few relatively sensibly upgraded Triumphs, and the odd crazy one as well.

The Triumph badge has been seen on some of the world's most stylish and best-loved popular cars. It is now owned by BMW.

Fitting a brake servo? Follow our step-by-step instructions

TRIUMPH
WORLD

www.kelsey.co.uk

OCTOBER/NOVEMBER 2006
No.70 £3.99
USA $7.15
CANADA $10.95

TR6 V8
Awesome 5.0-litre beast for road or track!

1971 Stag
First owner: Dr Kildare

1955 TR2
Founder of a dynasty

Dolomite Sprint: rolling restoration marathon

1947 Triumph Roadster
Unique and original example under the spotlight

Engineers & Engines
Ray Bates interviewed

Show reports
Full coverage of Stafford and Malvern events

From the Archives

The next step after having a GT6 is probably a TR6. The author has not yet bought his TR6, but has driven several and can feel the magnetic pull of its crisp lines and crisper exhaust note. This applies even more if they're creatively modified: the author was well impressed by this cheeky 5-litre V8 TR6 that he reviewed for Triumph World magazine.

Spitfire bonnet badge for the American market only – it would have looked inappropriate in the UK to have used an RAF roundel to connect a little 1147cc sports car directly to the machines that won the Battle of Britain. BMW now owns both the Triumph and presumably the Spitfire names – so will they have the nerve to use it?

buying the right Triumph: value for money

You have to be crystal clear about the reasons why you want a small Triumph. If you would enjoy getting involved in restoration or pottering, you can be much more flexible when looking for a car. If you have a MIG welder and a garage and would enjoy cutting out rusty panels and making and welding in new ones, then by all means buy and rescue a rusty car. However, if you just want to own and drive a Triumph, only buy the best. The general rule about buying the best one you can find is critical with these cars, because *it could cost three or four times the value of a good finished car to restore a bad one.*

SAVE MONEY – BUY A ZOBO OR A BOMB

Heralds, which were originally codenamed Zobo, are the least expensive of the flip-front Triumphs. If, again, you are looking for a hands-on hobby project car that needs work, they are available for well under £1,000. Between £1,000 and £2,000 should get you a running and fairly

solid but scruffy run-of-the-mill saloon with an MOT. Insist on an MOT before buying, by the way, unless the price is at scrap level.

From £3,000 to £4,000 will get you a nice saloon and into the convertible arena, possibly an older restoration, and also into some of the rarer models that will appreciate more. On a random winter Internet surf, we find a 1960 948cc saloon in nice condition for £4,500, and £2,750 gets a 1966 estate, which would be a very useful vehicle: if you didn't need to go anywhere far or fast, you could use that as a very economical daily car.

£6,000 gets us into buying a car from a dealer. At this level you're looking for no rust at all, and those on offer will mostly be convertibles. If you pay something like £8,000 for a Herald, you're going to get a fresh restoration and almost a new car – and somebody will have lost quite a lot of money, because it will have cost three times that much to carry out a half-decent restoration. But often, the labour doesn't come into the calculation because it

A Spitfire 1500 offers very good value for money. This particular example had just been expensively restored and was on sale for $7,000 Canadian – around £3,500. Tempting, as it was pretty well perfect.

would have been a hobby project. You don't really clock the hours of labour involved when you go skiing or sailing, because you expect to pay for hobbies, not to be paid for doing them. Quite of lot of hobby restorers just want to get rid of a freshly finished car for enough money to get on with the next one. Like a jigsaw, it's of no interest when it's finished.

Moving up a class to Vitesses, a tempting example at the time of writing was £2,500 for a scruffy red Mk II with overdrive, wire wheels and a sunroof – though that rather scruffy-looking drivable project would probably be a temptation best resisted unless it was very solid. At the £4,000 to £6,000 level you're looking at fairly good Vitesses. The premium for a convertible seems less strong than with Heralds, and the engine size and date doesn't

seem to matter too much. The 2000cc engine is torquier, but the earlier 1600cc is revvier and sweeter. Two concours Vitesses were on offer for £11,000 and an optimistic £20,000. Paying something between £8,000 and £12,000 for a virtually new Vitesse could make sense, because you certainly couldn't have one restored for that – although if you supplied the labour yourself for the fun of it, you could probably home-restore a Vitesse to a good level for £10,000.

Spitfires were originally known by the codename Bomb, and are plentiful and cheap. The later ones are generally even cheaper. The 1500cc engine shared with the MG Midget provides useful touring torque, but the favourite engine among the Spitfirati is the 1300.

For just a few hundred pounds we're looking at viable

The least favourite Spitfire among the cognoscenti is the later 1500, which is heavier, slower-revving and more modern. Try various models and engine sizes before deciding on your chosen period.

Spitfire Dick is in his nineties and still breaks up Spitfires as a paying hobby. He collected enough good parts to win concours prizes with his assembled parts collections.

restoration projects with holes in the floors, and if you're not keen on welding, many abandoned restoration projects are sold very cheaply at the magic 90 per cent level, with all the structural rust already repaired. Cars in pieces are worth very little. People do the big and difficult bits, and they – or their wives – get totally sick of the interminable boring last details and just give up, passing on a bargain to you or me. A few months of reassembly and a paint job, and we're driving a very nice car.

'Been standing for while, runs, £1095 ONO' is also worth a look and can probably be had for £500 worth of waved twenties. (Carry £20 notes rather than fifties, as they make a more impressive wad.)

Between £2,000 and £3,000 gets us a reasonable and drivable Spit, and above £4,000 they start getting nicer. Above £5,000 and we're getting older restorations, new paint, new engines and some of the more interesting cars: a 1969 1300 with 70,000 miles (112,000km) and a full history could be a nice buy at £5,000. We also have the option of buying from the trade. This means paying over the odds, but traders don't generally bother buying in rubbish, and with the small claims court as an option for back-up, you can get faults sorted out. Classic car traders are also more likely to be reasonably honest than mainstream second-hand car types.

There are also intriguing buys about, if you're patient and quick – how about £2,200 for a 1976 Spit with a Dolomite 1850 engine, overdrive gearbox and GT6 bonnet? That would go like stink until the head gasket blew.

On the subject of the GT6, this is the top of the small Triumph class. They are best treated as tourers than sports cars, though – the engine is heavy and too far forwards in a light car, and the handling on early ones is not up to the amount of power available. They're exquisitely pretty, and as in the E-Type, the coupé GT6 version of the Michelotti design is prettier than the convertible Spitfire, although there's nothing wrong with the lines of a Spitfire. The GT6 was often referred to as the 'poor man's E-type', and there's truth in that. Their desirability means they tend to start at £6,000 for something fairly good, rising to £9,000 and above for restorations or survivors: a 48,000-mile (77,000km) 1967 Mk I with no welding and its original paint sounds fairly priced at £11,500 – although with that one, you'd really have to tolerate the original and period-correct rear suspension, rather than sort it out.

Triumph-based kit cars offer some good deals and some good fun. The most frequently available ones are Gentries, which are replicas of the early 1950s MG TF. They're sometimes built on a Triumph chassis and sometimes on a custom chassis, which will be made of girders. They tend to sell for between £3,000 and £5,000 if functional, and a small fraction of that if unfinished. If buying an unfinished one, make sure that it uses an original Triumph chassis with a valid registration as a Gentry, or has been registered as a Gentry with a new chassis, or you'll have to go through a difficult, silly and expensive (£500) government test.

There are also the plan-built, plywood-bodied Burlingtons and JC Midges, which look more like the 1930s period than the 1950s. I write for *Kitcar* magazine, and I am the madman who built the first 6-cylinder, 2-litre, Vitesse-based Midge. After much of the usual hassle, the Vitesse rear axle was changed for a live axle from a Dolomite, on a custom linkage with a Panhard rod. You can do that on a kit car, although it would be a bit tricky on a Triumph body and chassis. It's certainly out of the purlieu of everyday modifications.

Burlingtons and Midges are cheaper than Gentries because they're more free-form in concept, and many have proportions that look grotesque. However, they can all be aesthetically saved with more plywood and a set of bolt-on hubs and 18in wire wheels.

ORIGINALITY

Mentioned elsewhere in this chapter is one car I would not modify – an £11,500 Mk I GT6 with 48,000 miles (77,230km) and its original paint. Any low-mileage, untouched, time-capsule survivor has intrinsic historic value and potentially substantial longer-term financial value, and should really be preserved. The rest of the remaining Triumph fleet is, however, fair game for an individual treatment, and there are still thousands of cheap old Triumphs out there to play with.

Some types of modification will definitely add value, such as a set of wire wheels or an extra carb fitted to a single-carb engine. Overdrive is a boon for nearly all Triumphs, but the best way to buy an overdrive set-up is to get the entire system from another Triumph, including the switch – which means either steering column electrics with the right extra stalk, or a gear lever with a thumb switch on it. Remember to keep intact everything of the old mechanicals that you take off, and present it in a box with the car when selling it.

Performance modifications generally probably won't pay you back, but within reason, they won't do any harm to values. Nearly all modifications are bolted on and can therefore be unbolted and removed, should the next owner be a purist.

Among the best vintage racing in the world is the Circuit des Remparts at Angoulême in France, where this delightful and obviously treasured early Spitfire was spotted.

This might look like an expensive postwar MG, but it's actually a Triumph-based Gentry kit car. Plenty were made, and scruffy ones in need of some love can be bargains. R. HAWKINS

FREE ROAD TAX

Many small Triumphs are free of road tax, which for some reason is a tax that is resented more than most. There is pleasure in not paying road tax, which is out of proportion with the amount saved: not paying it is also an annual and recurring pleasure. Pre-January 1974 is the current cut-off date for free tax.

The downside of this is increasing EU pressure for conformity, or as they put it, 'harmonization', and the free road tax means our classic car fleet is being singled out as a different class of vehicle. Regulation is creeping in already in that classics are banned from Paris, all German classics must be fitted with catalytic converters, and there's a risk that the UK will eventually be instructed by the EU to restrict the use of free-road-taxed classic cars to parades and going for repairs. Join a classic car club and push it to support the Fédération Internationale des Vehicules Anciens (FIVA) in fighting off approaching restrictions.

A Spitfire is quite a practical sports car, with a decent boot. A boot rack is also a good idea, but put the raised bar towards the front of the car – it's to stop luggage hitting your head, not to resist the car's fearsome acceleration.

Vitesses are seriously nice and useful cars, and are still quite affordable. The bodywork is still Herald apart from the front end, which keeps repairs cheap. P. BARLOW

The 2-litre Vitesse is the faster and more common option, but the 1600cc six is a very sweet engine that likes to rev. P. BARLOW

INSURANCE

It's wise to be clear about who and what the insurance industry is. Essentially, insurance companies are institutionalized gamblers, whose job is to get as much money in as they can and to pay out as little as they can. The borderline between squeezing you and defrauding you is a grey area, and wriggling out of paying a claim using a small-print technicality is a favourite trick.

You must declare in detail and in writing every tiny modification carried out on your car, without fail. Even a smaller steering wheel could be cited as a contributory cause to a collision if it had not been declared in writing or on a recorded and printed-out email to the insurance company.

You can opt for an agreed value policy, in which you might pay a higher premium, but you will get more of your money back with less hassle.

The classic car insurance world can afford to be more gentlemanly in its behaviour, as it has plenty of spare money. Hagerty has so far proved helpful and honest in my experience.

Observe the number of insurance ads in car magazines: as classic car enthusiasts we offer rich pickings. Our premiums remain usefully low because of strong competition between companies, but the claims on classic cars are almost zero. The main cause of general modern-car collisions and claims is inattention and stupidity, and having invested a great deal of time and money in our classic cars, we simply drive them carefully and don't cause collisions. We may drive fast, but we do not drive stupid fast, and paying attention while driving is enough to ensure that we make virtually no claims.

When somebody does hit your car, leave it where it is until you have pictures, and pin down any potential witnesses before they can leave. Always have paper and pen in the car, or a smartphone. It's not a bad idea to involve the police and not to get out of your car if anything is at all painful: that makes it an injury accident requiring a police presence, and if charges are laid against the other driver, this makes the blame crystal clear and the opposing insurance company can't slide out of paying.

You may be offered a derisory sum to write your car off: on a small Triumph, a damaged bonnet alone will probably make it uneconomical to repair. I've found it has worked in the past to dispute a low restitution offer by telling the insurance company that I will accept either my own valuation of the car, backed up by advertisement prices, or if they genuinely believe that a comparable replacement car can be bought for the price they offer, they are welcome to find and buy me another vehicle of the same model, condition and year. Otherwise I want their formal company address for the serving of a small claims court summons. If necessary you can pursue these at a very reasonable cost and without a lawyer, with a good chance of success. The limit for small claims in the UK is now £10,000, which covers most small Triumph models other than possibly a concours GT6. Just the serving of a summons often gets a result, because it says that you are serious and that it will be cheaper for them to give you a decent settlement than not to. It's personal for you, but it's just arithmetic for them.

Make the return of the salvage of your car part of any deal, because although repairs are not economically viable for an insurance company contracting an expensive body shop, they nearly always are for a private owner. Unofficially, there are also two levels of payment with body shops: unless there is a backroom deal in place, the price quoted to an insurance company for a repair is a lot higher than a cash quote for a private person.

Again, the Triumph chassis offers an advantage, because you can easily change a damaged flip front

The Vitesse chassis doesn't care whether it carries a Triumph body or a lightweight wooden one: after some twenty-seven years, this future Gentry is now approaching completion.
P. WOOD

for a secondhand replacement. You can also replace or repair a bent body tub as a winter project, and even if the chassis is twisted, you can repair or change that as well, although changing the chassis can raise legal and identity complications.

I bought my own GT6 in the 1980s for a few hundred pounds as an insurance write-off, because somebody had driven into the back of it. The back panel had crumpled in a fair bit, making it look pretty bad cosmetically, but the roof, the tailgate and the C-pillars were still straight.

Spitfire Dick has enough spares to last a thousand years! Joining the TSSC is an excellent idea, as many members are also hoarders and can help keep your Spitfire in fine shape.

It's a big help that there's no chassis at the back of a GT6 or a Spit to get bent, just soft bodywork, so within reason, damage is likely to be mostly cosmetic. I spent a day with a sledgehammer and a lump of hardwood, bashing the bodywork straight again until the tailgate lined up and latched perfectly, and then I skimmed a thin layer of filler over the remaining small wrinkles, and painted the back end in my driveway with a couple of spray tins from Halfords. I think one replacement tail-light and a new bumper finished off the repair, and it looked pretty good.

REGULATIONS

Triumphs of our type are in quite a good position as regards official paperwork and modifications, because they have a chassis. You can do what you like with the body as long as you more or less comply with 'Construction and Use' regulations, and you don't face the problems facing Mini and other modern-classic owners whose cars have a monocoque. If the monocoque on a Mini is cut, for instance by enlarging the speedo hole in the dashboard

to fit an airbox for a Weber, the car might, at its next MOT, be required to go through an Individual Vehicle Approval (IVA) test because of the alteration. Most MOT inspectors are sensible and would say that this was a stupid waste of time, but some may not.

In practical terms the traffic police have changed and are no longer petrolheads with encyclopaedic knowledge of the Construction and Use Act, so drivers of modified classic cars are probably less likely to be stopped than in previous years: you'll still get a pull if they're bored, but it will be curiosity rather than oppression, and it is certainly best responded to on that basis.

A 1970s acquaintance who drove a jacked-up drag-strip Zephyr with huge rear wheels used to be hassled regularly for illegally high rear lights, until he dangled red and yellow repeater bulbs on wires to the correct height, complying with the letter of the law – but the police are not stopping any Ford Focuses (or Foci), on which the rear light heights look to me blatantly illegal.

MOT tests are now optional for cars built before 1960, although for Triumphs this only means a few Heralds.

The expected engine in a Triumph-based kit car is a Spitfire or Herald, but you can usually jam in a six, and you definitely should. *R. HAWKINS*

Left-hand-drive Vitesses are very rare, as they weren't really exported to North America; this one came to Vancouver via Switzerland. *P. BARLOW*

UPGRADING LIGHTS

The lighting on Triumphs is all right at the front, although you need to keep all bulb holders properly earthed to retain the lights' full brightness. Herald, Spitfire and GT6 headlights can be upgraded with uprated bulbs to brighter alternatives, although the smaller Vitesse headlights might be trickier to uprate. Triumph rear lights are not up to modern standards, so fitting a rear red foglight or two at the back under the bumper and switching it/ them on in poor weather would be wise. A bright repeater LED brake light under the bumper would also be wise. Nearly all newish cars have third brake lights mounted high up in the back window, so putting them somewhere different so they stand out and attract more attention is what you're after. Adding a hazard warning light circuit would also be a good idea, an upgrade that is covered in the electrics chapter (Chapter 9).

Annual MOT tests are actually a good idea, even though it's superficially useful to postpone repairs until convenient, rather than having to deal with them every year by a specific date. I mostly live in British Columbia, where there is no annual testing other than emissions. For that reason I have put off repairing the rust on my runabout Mini for eight years, as a result of which it is now structurally dangerous and would disintegrate if involved in an accident, and I have had to stop using it. It would have failed a British MOT on minor sill and floor rust when I bought it, and I would have had to have repaired it. It may now be too far gone and might have to be scrapped, which would never have happened if it had had to be MOTed every year. Do you have the strength of mind to do rust repairs when you ought to, rather than when you have to? I strongly recommend that you take your Triumph through a voluntary MOT every year and pretend the repairs are compulsory, because that way you'll possibly avoid having to throw it away later.

It's an excellent idea to interrupt either the low-tension lead to the coil or the fuel-pump wire with a hidden or disguised switch, to deter thieves. This Jag overdrive switch would fool thieves, but only if they could read.

Most of the Triumphs restored at Randy Zoller's British Heritage Motorsports workshop are TRs, as the low value of Spitfires means high-level restoration makes no commercial sense.

One of the author's favourite cars was this very nice 1972 GT6, bought for a bargain price with minor rear body damage and repaired with a sledgehammer and some P38.

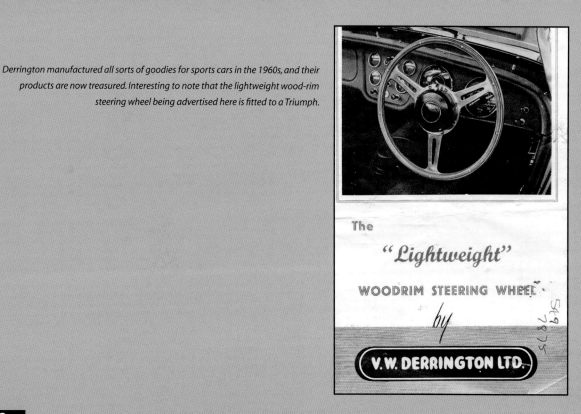

Derrington manufactured all sorts of goodies for sports cars in the 1960s, and their products are now treasured. Interesting to note that the lightweight wood-rim steering wheel being advertised here is fitted to a Triumph.

The "Lightweight" WOODRIM STEERING WHEEL by V. W. DERRINGTON LTD.

masterclasses

THE PHILOSOPHY OF PERFORMANCE

The Derrington company specialized in Triumph performance improvements in the 1960s. Designer Miles Fenton worked there sixty years ago, and gives us his advice on improving Triumphs. After some sixty-five years of fiddling with machinery to make it go faster, which included working at legendary Triumph performance outfit Derrington, and vintage racing success in his own special, Miles has isolated the single most important word in car performance: predictability.

Miles worked at Derrington in the 1960s when he was quite young, so he tackled whatever task came up, including sales and deliveries as well as engineering work on engines. He installed quite a lot of cams. Most of Derrington's cams were made by Ruddspeed, who were responsible for the fast Ford Zephyr engine used in the AC Ace before it evolved, or rather exploded, into the Cobra.

'Vic Derrington was a wily old man,' says Miles. 'Very cautious.' Derrington did have a simple flow bench,

though unlike most in those days, and the company was the acknowledged expert on Weber carbs, which Miles advises against incautiously using on small engines. 'The chokes are just too big, so you can't get any gas speed at slow rpm. They'll almost stall on takeoff, although they work a treat when you're flat out.'

The weekends were the high point of this job for Miles. Derrington had a lorry and a mobile workshop at all the major VSCC races, and they fixed anything that needed fixing, usually at panic speed before the next race. Exploded clutches would be sorted, and leaky fuel tanks brazed up (very carefully). Rather as in wartime, you tend to learn a lot very quickly if you want to survive. However, working during the week for a cautious man became dull, and Miles was happy to be poached by Paddy Gaston, who ran a similar operation and who also ran the fastest Sprite in the UK, bearing the number plate RAM 35. His concentrated experience with that BMC A-series engine can be usefully applied in many ways to other small British iron 4-cylinder overhead-valve engines, such as the 803cc

Miles dug up this photo of the Derrington truck at Silverstone back in probably 1959. He used to drive this beast there and back, staying overnight and sleeping up over the cab in a damp bedroll. M. FENTON

standard four from which our Herald-period engines are derived.

Miles also built a Riley-based special from scratch, applying all the experience he had absorbed from working with some of the top people of the time in racing and performance. However, the idea of predictability being the most critically important single aim of any automotive engineering procedure took a while to emerge.

Triumph Suspension

When it comes to Triumph suspension, the design flaw of the swing axles means major unpredictability at the back, combined with very good predictability at the front. It goes without saying that taming the wayward rear end is your first priority. My own solution to the problem, which was drastic but effective, involved replacing the whole rear end with a live axle from a Dolomite, on trailing arms, coilover shocks and a Panhard rod. This requires some fabrication, and the track ends up at 51in compared to the original 49in, but the propshaft and the wheels bolt straight back on, and unwelcome suspension surprises are over.

A live axle also raises the unsprung weight, which is undesirable, but the 100 per cent improvement in predictability is worth all the effort if you want to drive quickly and safely. That predictability is what I was aiming for, albeit subconsciously. Not many of us will want to get involved in such dramatic design and concept changes, though, so all I can suggest is to research the options for

The Fenton special: a Riley put together according to the theories developed during decades of hands-on involvement in vintage racing.
M. FENTON

improving stability with the existing design, such as lowering the diff, fitting a pivot to the spring, or using an extra lower spring restricting the movement of the main spring, to make the best of a bad job.

Discussing the Colin Chapman/Lotus suspension philosophy of soft springs and hard shocks, Miles tends not to agree with that approach, because you can't predict how a soft spring in a car will react, compared to a hard one. This probably partly stems from his racing experience with pre-war cars using André Hartford friction shocks (Miles once worked for André Hartford Shock Absorbers Ltd as well), because they only work within a very limited range of bump suppression. On big bumps they're simply useless. So you can see that soft springs combined with

A handsome little beast, it still thrives, and now changes hands for respectable amounts of money. A Vitesse chassis and mechanicals can also be persuaded to turn into a less ambitious but still amusing special. M. FENTON

A little gentlemanly supercharging not only makes a lightened car go like a greased squirrel, it also protects the internals by applying constant light pressure to the engine internals. M. FENTON

ineffective friction shocks would be potentially suicidal, while hard springs offer predictability and control. Miles advises that as you can now buy oil/gas tubular shock absorbers that are adjustable for both compression and rebound, you should do so.

Tyres

Miles shares my own enthusiasm for getting contact patch weight right, and cites a Graham Hill race of around 1961 in a BRM, at which somebody had inadvertently loaded the previous year's tyres into the truck. They were much narrower than the current year, and with the right contact patch weight for the car, on a very wet practice day he wiped the floor with everybody else on the track. Nowadays racing tyres are huge, but contact patch weight is kept high by massive aero downforce loading: without the aero gear, most F1 cars would crash before the first corner.

Miles also tends to run tyres with quite high pressures for early, cart-sprung cars. A hard tyre retains its shape and offers predictability. Again this comes from racing pre-war cars, where the tyres were narrow and hard, and didn't have much grip – but you could often go faster in a controlled slight drift than with higher but unpredictable grip. It's a different technique requiring skill and bottle, known as 'throttle steering,' but it's effective.

It doesn't apply to road cars so much, but if you take a lot of weight out of a car to make it go faster, you have also increased the percentage of undesirable unsprung weight – so rebalancing that percentage with alloy wheels, calipers and hubs becomes progressively more important.

Engine Development

Moving on to engines, we find history repeating itself. Master tuner from eighty years ago Freddie Dixon used six Amal bike carburettors on a 6-cylinder engine, looking for small bores and high gas speeds – which is exactly what V-performance.com in New York are now doing with modern Mikuni carbs for Triumphs.

The tendency for one engineering decision to create ten new problems is seen by Miles as a ripple effect, so he tends to think holistically about engine development, although his lip will undoubtedly curl at that word. Therefore he thinks about exhausts more than I would, because although he's well aware that standard exhaust systems can deal with states of tune well above anything we would normally use on a road car, bad exhaust design

can actively interfere with the rest of the engine. He likes David Vizard's idea of using a slightly bigger bore exhaust manifold piping than the port size, rather than matching the port exactly to the manifold. A step up in size of $1/16$in between port and manifold tubing does nothing to affect the outgoing gas, but it does interfere with any gas trying to go back into the cylinder: it acts as something of a non-return valve. The main exhaust bore should be as small as possible concomitant with no restriction, as smaller-bore tubing and higher gas speed mean more extraction effect and better breathing.

Moving inside the engine, the camshafts of the 1960s were nasty. They had very high lift with sharp shoulders on the lobes, and they gave the engine a rough idle and wore themselves and their related components out very quickly. There have been a lot of developments in cam design since those days, and of course everybody selling cams now has their own flow bench, or you don't buy their products. The days of 'Suck it and see' as a commercial performance research orthodoxy are long gone.

Lightening flywheels is usually done the wrong way, according to Miles. Taking weight off the whole face is 50 per cent a waste of time. It's the outer revolving mass you want to reduce, more than the general weight: the mass that causes the problem is located at the outside of the wheel, which is where you should remove the weight. The inner area near the crankshaft isn't a problem because you're not wasting much power spinning that up – it's the leveraged mass and inertia out at the edge of the flywheel that slows the engine acceleration down. Moderation is advised here for road engines, though, and you obviously can't mill anything off inboard of the outside edge of the clutch disc.

At the intake side of the engine, Miles has traditionally specialized in using SUs, although he appreciates that a set of existing Strombergs with a bit of internal polishing and smoothing can comfortably provide enough mixture, and enough is precisely what you need. With the SUs, Miles smooths and polishes the internals, grinds off any ledge before the jet, and adds a velocity stack to suck in air smoothly. His major advice on SUs is that the spindle holding the butterfly is a very bad aerodynamic shape and causes unwanted turbulence: it should be carved to the shape of a blade, with most of its material removed – it just has to remain strong enough to hold up the butterfly, so most of it can be carved away.

Miles is a great proponent of supercharging. You lose some energy in operating what is actually an air compressor, but you usually gain at least double the energy you've put in. He also says that supercharging to a gentlemanly level of 8–10lb is very protective of the internals of an engine, because there is constant pressure on all the internal bearing surfaces. There is no opportunity for slop to develop in bearings or bushes because the pressure is very rarely backed off – only under engine braking. With no forced induction and no constant internal pressure, and with the rotating components slopping back and forth all the time, any wear in the engine is made worse every time you back off the throttle.

Valve technology has developed a lot. Derrington used to offer two-angled valves and seats, which were cutting-edge technology in the sixties, but valves can have up to five angles now, and reputedly seven. Bigger and bigger valves have always been the trend, but Miles points out that you can still make the mistake of using valves that are too big for their surroundings. If part of a valve is almost touching the wall of the combustion chamber, the flow around quite a lot of it will be very bad, so a smaller valve would probably achieve increased gasflow and power.

He also likes lightening the valve train as much as possible with lighter rockers and lightweight tubular pushrods: it all contributes to the search for higher rpm while still avoiding valve bounce.

Another interesting idea from Miles is paying significant attention to the positive control of engine heat. Engines are better run hotter rather than cooler, and each engine has its own ideal temperature. With modern and usefully cheap thermostat controls that can be applied to both electric radiator cooling fans and to valves on oil coolers, you can establish your engine's most powerful (and therefore best) temperature on a track day by comparing lap times, and then stick to it.

THE AMERICAN PERSPECTIVE

Master mechanic and Triumph restorer Randy Zoller tells us what would be his ultimate small Triumph, and why. He has had the delightful advantage of modifying lots of his customers' cars at their expense rather than his own, which is an excellent and very cost-efficient way of finding out what works, and of collecting expertise.

Randy Zoller's Ultimate Triumph

Randy's personal ultimate Triumph has never been built, because as a restorer he spends all day fixing Triumphs, so the idea of spending his evenings fixing another Triumph has limited appeal. He does have a delightfully patinated, 400,000-mile (645,000km) TR250 as a personal car which

he fires up for long trips, but his fun car is a Morgan V8. It is an ill-tempered and brutish thing, but top fun.

There's also a V6 wedge-period TVR, sadly unused for some time, so Randy probably won't ever have the time or inclination to build a personal Triumph. However, speculating about what such a Triumph might be if he were to build one, that's a different matter.

Perhaps surprisingly, Randy's idea of the most desirable of the smaller Triumphs would be a 2-litre Vitesse. That's partly because they were only occasionally imported into the USA, so they're pretty rare. It's also because the twin-headlight bonnet with its frowning 'eyebrows' looks quite assertive, which in terms of styling, blends interestingly with the lightness of Michelotti's design and its delicate glasshouse.

A very close runner-up for Randy would be a Spit 6 – the GT6 drivetrain with a Spitfire bodyshell. Randy would pick a later body rather than earlier, as the Mk I lights are inadequate for driving at night. Later, pre-Karmann rear-end lighting updates, and the addition of more-round Lucas tail-lights to the old-school rear lighting, become more adequate from a safety viewpoint, but they're still a compromise – it all gets rather cluttered. But the dramatic 1970s Karmann styling and lighting update gets a thumbs-up from Randy.

He lives in San Diego, which has a pretty well perfect climate, so a convertible Vitesse is the likely choice, although the fine pillars supporting the roofs of the saloons are very pretty, and a full-length Webasto sunroof on a saloon is an excellent option.

External Appearance

Colour would be something dark, navy blue or BRG, with a top paint job and good enough preparation work to carry off dark paint, and the wheels would be four-spoke Revolutions or multi-spoke Panasports, similar to Minilites. Given that this is an ultimate and theoretical car, it might even have a set of sixty-spoke wire wheels with stainless spokes and hubs, and aluminium rims. These are expensive, but they are available from Motor Wheel Service (MWS) in the UK, and they are exquisite.

Still on the visual side, the seats would be black and leather-faced, as black leather tends to look better and better with age as it collects patina and texture. The dash and door caps would be refinished in a dark burr walnut veneer, book-matched, with many coatings of proper oil-based gleaming varnish, and a wood-rim Moto-Lita steering wheel with the wooden rim colour-matched to the dash veneer.

Racing certainly improves the breed, and it is also extremely useful for the learning curve of restorers and mechanics. Randy Zoller has been developing a successful racing TR4.

Mechanically

Mechanically the front suspension would remain essentially standard, and if it's in good condition it's just fine as it is. The only change would be to add Spax shocks, because they're fully adjustable and they work well on the rebound as well as in compression. There would be an anti-roll bar, and the springs would be lowered by no more than an inch or so.

At the back, the suspension would still use the transverse spring, but with the central swivel in late GT6 style, and the axles would have constant velocity joints rather than Rotoflex.

There would be a five-speed gearbox rather than an overdrive – either a Type 9 Ford or a Tremec. Both have useful ratios, and both will comfortably handle the engine's potential output. He wouldn't use the TR6 four-speed and overdrive option because the Ford/Tremec option is cheap, easily available, smaller, lighter, simpler and more reliable, and a good O/D TR6 box should really be in a TR6.

The Engine

The engine would be moved backwards in the chassis for better balance, but its state of tune wouldn't be extreme – it wouldn't even have an aluminium head. He would build it to something like 140bhp, with a similar torque number. The crank would be standard, but the rods would be billet and the fastenings made by ARP. That doesn't get you any more power, but it does mean you can 'let rip' a little without worrying as much about over-revving the engine. The cam would be a 290, and the rockers would run a 1.65:1 ratio with roller tips. The head would be port-matched and ported, and the exhaust a six-into-one. The starter would be a new high-powered one, the dynamo would become a small, powerful, single-wire alternator, and the battery would be a small, light, powerful racing item.

Every peripheral component – flywheel, water pump, pulleys – would be lightweight aluminium, and the whole rotating assembly would be balanced.

Perhaps the most surprising is Randy's choice of carbs – rather than SUs or big sidedraught Webers, he would use three Strombergs: for the 2-litre engine he likes the triple CD150 1½in Strombergs, or a pair of CD175 1¾in Strombergs is good as well. For the 2.5-litre engine, he likes triple CD175s.

TRIUMPH LEGEND KAS KASTNER

In a happy synchronicity, while looking around in a little automotive bookshop in Los Angeles, I came across an official Triumph publication, the *Competition Preparation Manual for GT6 and Triumph 2000*, written in period by Triumph legend Kas Kastner.

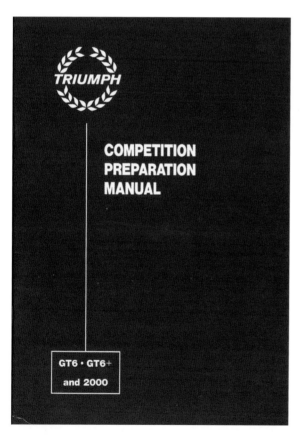

This Triumph-published competition guide for the GT6, GT6+ and Triumph 2000, written by Kas Kastner, turned up in an obscure motoring bookshop in Los Angeles.

Kas is still very much alive and kicking, and sells assorted books from his website www.kaskastner.com, which is well worth a visit.

Most of the information is for preparing the cars for racing and is therefore not really about 'everyday' modifications, but while you've got the cylinder head off anyway...

The Engine

The block should be decked and about 0.012in milled off, to achieve zero clearance with the top of the lowest piston at top dead centre. The rest of the pistons are matched to that piston height, to be flush with the block at TDC. The standard head gasket is 0.038in thick. Deglaze the cylinder walls, thoroughly clean out the oil galleries, and change the core plugs for new ones, which should be glued in place.

Magnaflux the crankshaft, and balance it with the front pulley fitted after cleaning out the oilways thoroughly. When fitting the crank, torque up the main bearings to 65lb ft.

The standard rods are strong enough for racing and don't need to be replaced. They can be lightened at the top of the little end, and at the joints where the rod bolts go through, and at the top and bottom of the big end circle. Get rid of any sharp edges or lumps, which could start a crack. Shot-peen the rods to relieve stress, and carefully clean out the used shot afterwards.

The standard pistons are also good enough for competition. You can radius the bottoms, balance their weights and polish them. Use cold plugs and avoid lean mixtures or excessive ignition advance, to protect the pistons. The standard piston rings are also good for racing: the top one is chrome and very tough, the middle one just needs to be the right way up, and the oil control ring is also good. The ring gap should be 0.012in.

The sump can be baffled for braking with a couple of plates going across, leaving a gap underneath.

Three camshaft choices are available: standard, road/race and race. End float should be 0.004in to 0.008in. Standard cam timing is fine and is recommended unless one is obsessive about every last bhp. Cam lube on initial start-up is critical.

Cylinder Head

Skimming 0.050in off the head achieves a compression ratio of 10.2:1, which is suitable for road and road/track use with premium fuel. For racing, taking 0.075in off the head gets 11:1, which is needed to match a race cam. Porting should aim for a port bore diameter of 1.3in, and the lump around the inlet valve should be removed. The ports should be matched to the inlet and exhaust manifolds. The port surface should be smooth but not polished.

If the head and block are skimmed and a high-lift cam is used, be sure to shim the rocker-shaft pedestals to compensate. Remember to drill a hole in the shim to match the oil delivery hole beneath it. Standard pushrods are fine. Standard valve springs will bind with a high-lift cam. The tops and bottoms of the springs should be polished to avoid fretting. The valves can usefully lose some material around the base of the shaft.

Fuel and Ignition

The standard Strombergs are fine for racing. It's worth cleaning up and polishing the castings, and fitting velocity stacks is effective. Port-match the carbs to the inlet manifold. Replace the mechanical fuel pump with an electrical pump wired directly to the ignition for reliability and safety – cutting the ignition cuts the fuel supply. Use thick and expensive plug leads, but the rest of the ignition system is fine if it is in good condition. The exhaust manifold should run to a single 2in exhaust pipe. (The use of twin pipes has been found to reduce back pressure too much, with a power loss of 6bhp.)

Radiator shrouding is critical – the path between the radiator and the front air intake must be airtight.

Gearbox and Transmission

The standard gearbox is acceptable for racing, but the nylon grommet on the gear lever should be replaced with a new one turned up to the same shape in aluminium. Oil should be 90 weight. The standard clutch is also all right for racing, and so is the flywheel, although it can be optionally lightened – but not so much that it warps with heat.

The standard differential is also good enough, although the best ratio in general is probably 3.89:1 for most circuits.

The half-shafts are not up to the job. It used to be possible to get hardened racing half-shafts, but that would have been in 1969. It is recommended that the shafts are replaced every five races.

Suspension

At the front, the castor should be set at 3.5 degrees. The front wheels should toe in by $1/16$in. Camber should be set at ¾ to 1¼in, depending on the oversteer characteristics of each car.

The rear spring should be de-arched to achieve a rear camber of 3.5 degrees negative.

The wheelbase should be set at 83in. The radius arms can be bent to clear fat tyres, but aluminium blocks must then be made to compensate for the loss of length. The rear wheels should toe out by $1/16$in.

The shrouding in this case is fairly important, as the engine in this GT6 is 5 litres rather than 2 litres, so the cooling system needs all the help it can get.

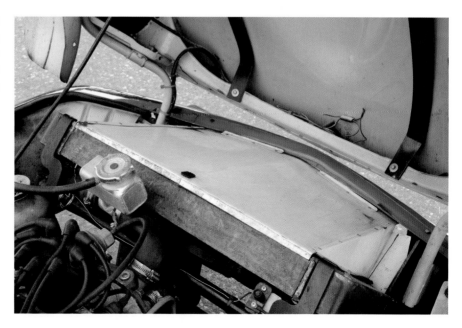

There is a great deal of pleasure to be derived from taking a rusty old piece of junk and transforming it into a gleaming and muscular work of engineering art. PATTONMACHINE

3

Triumph engines

Triumph themselves were historically tempted to play about with the performance of the small Herald/Spitfire engine, and a Stage 1 engine conversion was mooted, although it was never offered for sale. It would have featured a pair of Solex carbs and better inlet and exhaust manifolds, with a putative output of 70bhp. There was also a legendary Stage II kit sold, but in very small numbers indeed, so it's extremely rare. It comprised an eight-port cylinder head, twin Webers, a cheeky cam and an extractor manifold, and it would have produced respectable power.

The idea of fitting a later and larger 1500cc Spitfire engine to an earlier car may seem an obvious choice, and it does indeed bring an increase in torque, but if you want to drive fast, the 1500 is not the ideal engine. It has a long stroke and is not happy with high revs. The noise and feel of the 1500 engine above 5,000rpm is simply unpleasant, and it's much more suitable for cruising and ambling about. The extra torque makes it more pleasant around town as well. The Triumph tune manual and catalogue

suggested that they had some very good insight into modifying the 1500 engine, the most important point being the use of larger bearings so that the crankshaft didn't flex as much.

It would be reasonable to say that the great majority of Triumph enthusiasts like the 1296cc (1300) engine best. Here are the actual numbers:

- The rarer Mk I and Mk II Spitfires with the 1147cc engine initially sported 63bhp at 5,750rpm, and 67lb ft of torque at 3,500rpm, and then 67bhp at 6,000rpm
- The Mk III with the 1300 engine achieved 75bhp, and 75lb ft at 4,000rpm, although in 1973 power was reduced to 63bhp at 6,000rpm with torque of 69lb ft at 3,500rpm
- The 1500 Spitfire engine made 71bhp at 5,500rpm (US spec 53bhp) and 82lb ft at 3,000rpm

In terms of actual performance, there's not much in it, but the feel of the engines is quite different.

ENGINEERING IMPROVEMENTS

Purists as well as less committed Triumphistas will like the idea of uprating their cars with pieces of other Triumphs, and there are one or two options for this. The later GT6 cylinder head is based on the TR5 design and is an improvement on earlier 6-cylinder heads. More dramatically, and retaining the same stamped engine number, you can fillet a 2-litre six block and replace its crank and rods with the longer-stroke 2500cc items from a TR5/6-series car. Optionally and with some transmission tunnel and chassis clearance modification, you can also use the larger and stronger gearbox that comes with TRs.

The first task in the hunt for more power is to pull the head off and see if it has been fitted with hardened exhaust valve seats. If not, this needs to be done, and it makes sense to improve the breathing of the head at the same time.

Porting is the process of enlarging and smoothing the walls of the inlet and exhaust ports in the head. The surface should be smooth but not polished to a very shiny finish, as it then tends to condense the fuel out of suspension, losing power.

Match-porting is making sure that the diameters of the inlet and exhaust manifold ports are exactly matched to the head ports to avoid a step that disrupts gas flow.

Skimming is the process of milling some material off the bottom surface of the head, partly to make sure it's completely flat to avoid head gasket problems, and partly to raise the compression ratio to achieve more power. The cylinder block can also be checked for flatness, and skimmed or decked for higher compression. A compression ratio of 9.5:1 will require higher-octane pump fuel but will provide good power.

Value for Your Money

Here's a thought: if you put your engine-improvements budget into lightening the car, you might just get more practical performance per pound spent.

Camshafts

A cammed engine sounds nasty on idle, although that nastiness can be music to the ears of those who like fast cars. A high-lift cam also feels lumpy and uncooperative at low rpm, but when it sorts itself out and comes 'on cam' as the revs rise, it cleans up its behaviour, starts getting lots of gas through, and really sings. A 280 cam would be a suitable slightly cheeky profile for a road car, and the TR5's mildly insolent 150bhp cam is a recommended fast road cam profile for any 6-cylinder engine.

A suitable camshaft is a useful and reasonably economical everyday mod. Performance camshafts have higher and more dramatically shaped lobes, which essentially open the valves further, letting more air and fuel into the engine. There's no formal structure for the naming of cams: they tend to be described as 'fast road', 'rally' and 'race', or derivatives thereof. Fast road cams will improve breathing and contribute to extra power, but will still allow the engine to idle fairly smoothly and will retain some torque at lower revs.

The further you go with a cam, the more power you achieve, in concert with other mods, but the less smoothness and tractability. A really serious cam will make the engine spit and almost misfire at idle, and will possibly even bog down at low revs as the torque or grunt of the engine is compromised, but once the engine is howling, it will throw plenty of fuel and air down the ports and get serious power at 4,000 or 5,000rpm. The question is, how often will you be flat out and keeping the engine at the edge of the red section on the tacho? A full race cam is actually something of a disadvantage unless you're actually racing.

So where do you want your power band? 1,000–3,500rpm is good for shopping; 2,000–5,000rpm is good for a sports car; a power band restricted to 3,500–6,500rpm starts to become undrivable in traffic. Variable valve timing as in K-series or Honda Vtec engines gets good power from 1,000rpm to 8,000rpm, but with Triumphs we're still in the automotive Bronze Age and stuck with just one fixed cam profile.

Lighter cars need less low-end torque: the A-series Mini engine going into my very lightweight Mini-Marcos relies on its relatively larger 1100cc capacity (larger than 1000cc, anyway) for torque and shopping, but looks to its frisky Cooper S cam for power from 4,000–6,000rpm at playtime. Of course the whole car only weighs about 1,000lb (450kg), so the power-to-weight ratio means that 65bhp at 5,500rpm will be quite lively!

A related option, which can be used on its own or in carefully chosen combination with the cam profile, is high-ratio rockers. These change the leverage ratio with which the rocker pushes the valve into the cylinder. A frequently used ratio is 1.5:1. For every millimetre the pushrod pushes the pushrod side of the rocker up, the valve side goes down 1.5mm. Randy says, 'As it turns out, the stock ratio is 1.55:1 but I actually recommend the 1.65:1

ratio in conjunction with the 290 degree Newman cam, as it bumps the valve lift up considerably, which lets the cam work better at high rpm.'

If fitting new rockers, it's a good upgrade to go to roller rockers, which have a little roller bearing on the tip, reducing friction and allowing the use of modern synthetic oils without rocker wear. In the USA in particular, Randy recommends www.goodparts.com as a source of manifolds as well as quality roller rocker arms.

A Vernier cam pulley offers fine adjustment of the cam timing, and if you're putting any serious money in and extracting serious power, accurate timing is obviously going to get the very best out of a serious cam. The standard timing methods will be fine with a fast road cam. Increasing the lift gets you more power, and more duration – the amount of time when the valve is open – and it raises the rpm at which max power is achieved.

Long duration also means overlap, which is when both the intake and the exhaust valves are briefly open at the same time. Raw fuel goes right through the engine, and some escapes unburnt through the exhaust. Wasting fuel doesn't matter when we're racing, if it gets us another few bhp.

There are also consequences to the valves being pushed further into the cylinder, because eventually they will hit the pistons. Any change in the cam or rocker system would obviously mean the engine has to be revolved by hand to see if any valves hit any pistons. It's not a terminal problem provided the engine is turning by hand – pistons can have valve pockets milled out in their tops, although that reduces the compression: swings and roundabouts.

Valve springs are affected by rocker ratios as well. More is demanded from them, and there's a chance of coil binding, during which the spring is squashed completely flat and becomes a solid steel tube rather than a spring. Again, if that's happening the engine will jam when you try to turn it by hand, or if the engine is started, the rocker or rocker post will break. Higher-performance springs generally need to be thinner but stronger to avoid valve bounce at high rpm. It's also possible to mill out a deeper spring seat in the head to allow more room for movement.

There's usually some negative payback from increasing power, and in this case it's increased wear from faster and further valve movement, and lost power through higher mechanical resistance.

When buying a cam, choose a respected name. If you can buy from experienced Triumph people, so much the better. Ask what the hardness is: it should be more than sixty on the Rockwell C scale – you shouldn't be able to mark it with a file. If the shop doesn't know the hardness, go somewhere else.

Internals

Forged pistons and steel conrods are very nice, and that sort of engineering is pleasing to petrolheads. However, in some ways disappointingly, Kas Kastner says that standard Triumph pistons and conrods are good enough for racing, so there's no real need to go and buy any fancy ones for a road car.

The crankshaft, head, rods and pistons can be taken from a 2.5-litre engine and fitted to a 2000 block for a visually undetectable power increase – but the gearbox and diff won't take it for long. Conversion to the bigger 2.5 litre gearbox and differential is possible but brings its own complications.

Given the visibly neglected state of the engine, this piston doesn't look bad at all, and all the piston rings are still in one piece. However, the engine will probably need a rebore and new pistons.

With the questionable quality of some aftermarket replacement parts, it's wise to use ARP fixings on critical components such as big-end and main-bearing cap nuts and bolts.

This bearing is not only worn, but has been gouged by some bit of grit or swarf. Better filtration after a major clean-up will help to reduce that sort of damage.

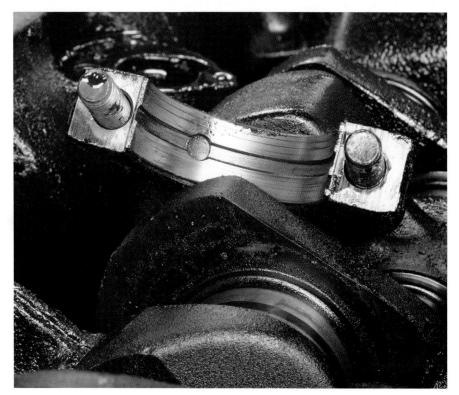

If a 2.5-litre engine is used, the 2-litre sump or oil pan must be installed in order to clear the steering rack and underside of the bonnet as the GT6/Vitesse sump is about an inch shallower. However, it will have to be modified to clear the crankshaft weights. Randy has an effective if brutal solution to this problem: he just applies heat where the sump fouls the crankshaft, and hammers it out until it clears.

Bores

If the engine is generally a bit smoky and uses oil, a likely cause is bore wear (if you get just blue oil smoke on the overrun, that's more likely to be valve-guide wear). Remove the head, and feel the top of the bore. If an edge can be felt by clicking your fingernail upwards towards the top of the bore, you need a rebore to cut the cylinder back to fresh, even metal, and then you need a set of new, slightly bigger pistons.

This is a machine shop job. You can either bore out the cylinders by the minimum necessary to get a good surface, in which case you may be able to do this again when you've worn the bores out again, or you can go for a one-off overbore, fit significantly bigger pistons, and get more capacity and more power.

Rocker Oil Feed Pipes

Adding a rocker oil feed pipe is a bad idea. It reduces the oil pressure and flow to expensive and critical crankshaft components, and improves pressure and flow to cheap and easily replaceable rocker shaft components. The threaded drilling and the plug on the head are to do with production casting methods and have nothing to do with oil feed, although the drilling opens into an oil gallery. Kas Kastner personally told me that extra external oil feeds are nonsense. Randy Zoller agrees, saying that he would take it one step further and state that he believes it actually does harm as it diverts oil pressure away from the crankshaft, especially at high rpm. He would also recommend bumping up the oil pressure slightly on a high performance engine by shimming or replacing the oil pressure relief valve spring.

Fasteners

Buying new old stock or Original Equipment Manufacturer (OEM) parts for a Triumph is an option that ran out a long time ago. Some of the available replacement parts are good, but some are rubbish. The way to find out if a cheap new cylinder head bolt is sufficiently hardened and free of

If the oil isn't changed regularly, this is the sort of filth that builds up inside the engine. It's surprising that an engine will still run in this condition, but Triumphs are tough old beasts.

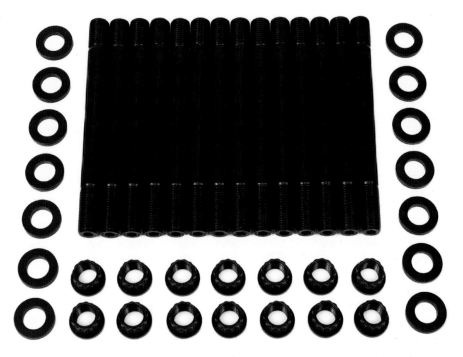

It costs about £60 for a set of ARP head studs and nuts for a GT6 engine. Not unreasonable, and you know what you're getting.

manufacturing flaws is to fit it to your pride and joy, and then drive it and hope for the best.

The cost of using ARP or similar uprated and guaranteed strong bolts where possible has to be worth it: big-end (rod) bolt sets from ARP are about £60.

Peripherals

Engine peripherals offer some room for improvement. The less weight and the less revolving weight the better, so anything you can change for a smaller and lighter version is a little improvement. This applies to flywheels, water pumps, pulleys and so on.

When you look at any Triumph with a view to buying it, you want to see clean oil inside the rocker cover. During your ownership, the oil should be changed religiously every 3,000 miles (5,000km).

High-torque starter, more efficient and powerful than the old-school Bendix style. It gives the option of a smaller and lighter battery.

Olivier Martineau's Engine Spec

1493cc
Pertronix ignition
Silicone plug wires
Hot spark plugs
Dual H4 SU carbs with custom needles and springs
K&N air filters
Exhaust manifold mandrel-bent stainless steel, into stainless-steel exhaust with Borla silencer
AC Delco alternator conversion
Compressed re-cored radiator
Estimated 75bhp

Cooling

Electric water pumps are more efficient than belt-driven ones, and the same applies to electric cooling fans mounted on the radiator. Electric pumps and fans should be relayed, and the radiator should be shrouded to ensure that it works as well as possible – stopping leaks of potentially cooling air is worth a big effort.

Sensors for aftermarket electric fans of the Kenlowe type should be mounted in the lower hose, not the top one. The sensors need to be measuring cooling water, as they can't get a temperature reading from steam. When somebody has made this mistake and terminally

Olivier Martineau has fitted a fairly powerful fan behind the radiator and has removed the original mechanical fan on the front of the engine.

barbecued their engine as a result, you can actually smell the burnt engine as you drive past. (It was a TR engine in a Morgan.)

Fans should be mounted on the inside of the radiator and should be pulling rather than pushing air, because the conditions behind the rad are generally drier and warmer. It's an electric motor, after all.

The radiator should be bigger and fitted with more cores. A hotted-up engine is also a hot engine – more performance means more heat as well.

New, aftermarket high-torque starter motors are a good idea. They are lighter, work better and use less power, which in turn would allow a smaller and lighter battery in cars where weight really matters. These hi-torque starters tend to be a universal Nippon Denso starter with mounting rings designed to fit specific applications.

Aluminium rocker covers offer a minimal weight-saving over the standard steel pressing, but they are stiffer and less likely to leak around the edges. I'd have to admit, however, that the main reason for fitting one is that they look nicer than the standard cheap tin job.

For an engine used regularly for hard or track-day driving, it's a good idea to baffle the sump, which means

Even basic radiator shrouding helps to keep incoming cool air coming through the radiator rather than escaping round the sides.

49

A-level rad shrouding on a TR6. The radiator is aluminium as well, which allows bigger tubes and a tough welded structure. Polished stainless sheet is hard to work with, but pretty when finished.

fitting plates to restrict the slopping around of oil inside the crankcase. The oil-pressure warning light is quite often in reality a chequebook warning light, because if the bearings are starved of oil for any more than a very brief period, they will be toast – and burnt toast at that. Under road and fast-road conditions, the oil in the sump slops around quite a lot, but the oil feed pipe is almost always still in the oil. Having said that, there's an amusing but potentially expensive corner local to me that involves about 300 degrees out of the 360-degree compass: it's an on-ramp to a highway that goes from north round to west through east and south, going clockwise after a bridge, and it's smooth, evenly surfaced and quite fast. I tend to push my road-going Mini round there pretty hard just for fun, but a friend pointed out that by about three-quarters of the way round, my oil pressure had dropped to zero because centrifugal force had pushed all the engine oil to the timing end of the engine and there was no oil in the pump. For a single corner and 100 yards, no worries, but under racing conditions with constant and extreme braking and cornering, baffling the sump will keep the bottom of the oil pipe in some oil.

Oil cooling is always good and prolongs engine life, not least because it means there is more oil in the system to absorb heat. An oil thermostat should be used to make sure the oil is actually getting up to the right temperature, though, as too-cold engines wear quickly. The TVR Sagaris

A remote oil filter kit allows the use of better modern filters with a non-return valve to stop drainage and to avoid the 'death rattle' of an engine started with an empty old-style filter.

The remote filter is often combined with an oil cooler, which adds capacity and certainly helps during hard use. This one is fitted beneath the engine: excellent airflow and nice cool air, but possibly slightly vulnerable.

This GT6 engine is fitted with a remote spin-on oil filter in place of the original tin bucket and paper filter. Spin-on filters have internal flaps to stop the oil draining back down into the sump, protecting the bearings on starting up. Adding an oil cooler is also easy once the remote system is fitted.

comes with a specific warning not to give it any revs until the oil is up to temperature. There is a minor extra weight penalty with an oil cooler, hoses and an additional pint or so of oil.

Fuel Pumps

Triumphs are fitted as standard with an exceptionally reliable mechanical fuel pump; this also comes with a useful priming lever, which can save a lot of churning of starter motors after fallow periods. The standard pump provides sufficient fuel volume and pressure for quite a high level of tune, but people sometimes fit an electric SU fuel pump.

These are also reliable, but they do have a working life. When retirement approaches, the SU pump gives you a helpful warning of its impending demise by packing up, and then starting up again and carrying on for a few more weeks or months, once you've hit it with the handle end of a screwdriver. This is known as percussive maintenance. Eventually the pump will pack up for real, although it can often be brought back to a full and productive second childhood via the cleaning, setting and lubrication of its contact points. The diaphragms can also fail, particularly if they're old and subjected to nasty modern fuel. You can

also opt for an electronic operation of the same pump, although that can't then be fettled or productively hit with a screwdriver. My Bentley project will run with twin SU fuel pumps, one with points and one with electronics.

The positioning of the fuel pump is also important – if you get vaporization with a mechanical or electric pump mounted in the hot engine bay, try relocating it to the boot or under the car, or supplementing it with another remote pump.

Exhaust Manifolds

This might be rather disappointing to hear, but performance exhaust manifolds and systems are mostly cosmetic and musical. You have to carry out some fairly dramatic work on the rest of the engine before you exceed the capacity of the standard exhaust system to deal with its exhaust gases.

However, let's assume that you might get serious about tuning later and are thus entitled to a fancy exhaust. Ideally, all the primary pipes of the manifold or header would be matched in length. A six-into-one manifold with a single collector box would get you more bhp higher up the rpm range, and two three-into-ones with two collector boxes would yield more low-end torque. Too free-flow

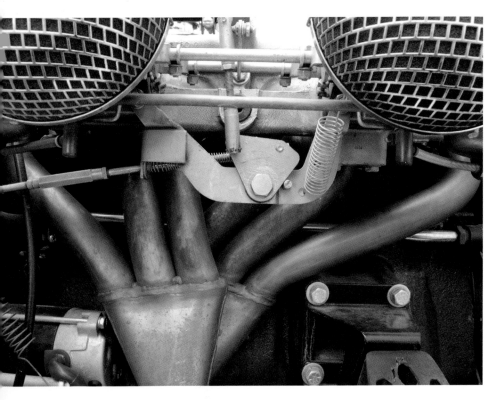

The Spit 6 has a nice three-into-two-into-one exhaust manifold. Theoretically this achieves more torque than a six-into-one, but on a road car the difference would be hard to define.

This four-branch exhaust manifold is probably overkill, as the engine has only one Stromberg and is not much of a monster. One point to note is that performance exhausts are usually thicker and last much better than thin standard systems.

Beneath the white San Diego Spit 6 mentioned in the case studies chapter is a pretty but possibly power-reducing set of tailpipes. One small-bore pipe promoting high gas speed will do the job.

a system, according to Kas Kastner, will lose back pressure and 6bhp.

Performance manifolds are also known as 'extractors' because the slug of exhaust gas expelled from the cylinder leaves a vacuum behind it, which helps to suck the next charge into the cylinder. If your exhaust piping is too big, gas speed will be slow, and that extraction effect will be reduced. Logically, a small-bore system will work better. The aesthetics are important for a sports car, though,

and a major reason for enjoying a Triumph straight six is the delightful exhaust chords, particularly from the rev-happy 1600cc Vitesse. A six-into-two branch manifold with a standard exhaust system is probably the optimum Triumph exhaust, although if you do want more of an auditory presence, it might be worth experimenting with small high-performance silencers that will still provide some back-pressure. A pea-shooter silencer and tailpipe on a 1600 Vitesse will work well and sound excellent.

There's a lot to be said for keeping it simple. This Spitfire has retained its original single Stromberg carb, with a free-flow air filter.

FUELLING

Carburettors

The first thing that Triumph enthusiasts generally do when it comes to improving the fuel system is to bin the Strombergs and fit SUs or something bigger. The established knowledge seems to be that Strombergs are good on economy and for emissions, but not for power. Having been a Triumph owner and enthusiast off and on since I was seventeen years old, I vaguely assumed this to be the case, but was astonished when Triumph restorer and racer Randy Zoller said he would fit three Strombergs to his theoretical ideal engine as a matter of choice. When asked to elaborate, he also said that two 175 Strombergs were just fine for any Triumph engine up to 2500cc.

Having thought about it for a few seconds, the inescapable conclusion is that if Strombergs are good on fuel and good on emissions, that means they're more efficient than SUs at most roadgoing throttle openings. I must admit that looking back over many years of driving Triumphs with Strombergs, I've never felt the need to change them apart from when the diaphragms have failed. Here's Randy on Strombergs:

I prefer the Strombergs because they have a lower profile thus making bonnet clearance better, and they have positive throttle shaft seals, integral float bowls and slightly faster response due to the positive diaphragm seal. Plus, when you have a triple set-up, you in effect have one carb that was jetted for three cylinders, now providing fuel and air for two cylinders. In a high performance application, the jetting turns out to be just about right without having to fiddle too much with them.

It's certainly true that the diaphragm in a Stromberg needs to be in good condition and that alternative performance parts for them are less easily available than they are for SU carbs, but given this fresh information – unless you're ahead of me and already know this – the smart move would be to work with the carbs that are on the engine in front of you, rather than automatically and expensively changing everything.

The only caveat to the Stromberg theory would be for seriously extreme engines requiring the dyno-based needle substitution and re-jetting of triple carbs: there is more experience available and there are more tuning parts available for SUs.

It has to be said that triple SUs do look sweet, but you would have to enjoy weekend fettling, as keeping them balanced would require some patience.

The Vitesses and GT6 that have passed through my hands have always had standard twin Strombergs, and to be honest I've never felt the need to change them, other than changing to K&N air filters rather than the potentially restrictive Triumph tin box.

V-performance swear by using sets of Mikuni carbs originally intended for large Japanese motorcycles, although bike carbs are designed for 13,000rpm rather than 4,000rpm.

Stromberg, Zenith and even Amal carb service kits and spares are still available from Burlen, who still make SU carbs. If you fancied a set of high-gas-speed period bike carbs, Amals are what you'd be looking for.

As with ignition timing, accuracy with carbs is crucial. The linkages between twin carbs must be perfectly set so that they both open at exactly the same time. This can be both measured and listened to – a straw between your ear and the opening of the carb is surprisingly effective at balancing, and is the old-school way.

Using carbs in pairs gets a better flow to each cylinder, with the maximum power via carbs being available through providing a single choke to each cylinder: this is why pairs of Webers or sets of four bike carbs for Spitfires are popular. But they are not necessarily successful in a car that's used for shopping as well.

It would be worth making the effort to use fat air tubing to direct cool air to the carbs from low down in the engine bay. You don't get any real ram pipe effect at road speeds,* but the cooler the incoming air, the more oxygen and therefore the more potential power there is in it, and also

anything you can do to avoid fuel vaporization and summertime bad hot starting is worth doing.

On all carbs, a well sorted and secured throttle return spring (or preferably springs) is critically important. Failures in that department, to my personal knowledge, have resulted in a Marcos disintegrating after a 120mph (190km/h) racetrack crash, and a 7-litre dragster Mini crashing upside down into a ditch at full power. One driver limped away, the other didn't.

It's very unlikely that you will generate enough fuel demand to overwhelm the standard fuel-supply piping, but for seriously powerful cars it would be worth going up a size if you were replacing it anyway.

The intake manifold on earlier sixes resembles a log, and trees are not the first objects that come to mind when considering smooth airflow. Frequently, good engineering looks good and bad engineering looks bad, and that certainly works for manifolds, both inlet and exhaust. If you can't visualize a smooth gas-flow path through a manifold, then neither can the gas.

You wouldn't normally go down from twin carbs to

*The exception to that is with speeds approaching 200mph (320km/h). A friend who has ridden his 1979 Triumph Trident streamliner to just over 200mph at the Bonneville Salt Flats says that his ram air system works a treat above 150mph (240km/h).

This piston is rather less than all right. This is the sort of damage caused by pre-ignition and detonation. It's frequently caused by the timing being too advanced: the mixture is exploding rather than burning. Knock sensors in computer-controlled engines retard the timing to prevent it.

a single carb, but if you have a Herald or a single-carb Spitfire, a much more plug-and-play experience involving minimal weekend tuning and fiddling would be to upgrade to a single larger carb instead of a pair. Either a bigger 2in SU or a Weber such as a 38DGAS would provide as much mixture as a Spitfire engine can handle. I'll be trying both of those on my slightly cheeky 1100cc Marcos engine, and will pick the one that feels better. Some of this is just subjective.

The volume of air that a carb can process and that an engine will suck in is measured in 'cubic feet per minute', or CFM. Ballpark maximum figures for the amount of air a Triumph engine takes in are as follows – 1300cc, 150CFM; 1600cc, 200CFM; 2500cc, 300CFM. That's at around 6,000rpm, so it's the absolute maximum that's going to be needed on the road.

A single HS4 SU can handle 133CFM, and an HS6, 210CFM. An HIF44 does 240CFM. In pairs, that's 266 CFM, 420CFM and 480CFM.

Each sidedraught 40DCOE Weber twin-choke can handle 350CFM with 36mm venturis and 480CFM with 38mm venturis.

So we can see that a 1300cc Spitfire engine that will use 150cu ft of air is more than adequately served by a pair of small SUs, and there's nothing to be gained by fitting bigger carbs – the bucket is full already and you can't get any more in. There's also the matter of reducing gas speed by providing a pointlessly bigger diameter of pipe, or by adding more pipes, to process the same amount of gas.

The only upside of fitting an oversized Weber and then jetting it down to SU performance is that, if you have later plans for other serious engine mods, it will be relatively quick and easy to re-jet for more power.

The *stoichiometric* mixture of petrol and air is the exact amount of air required to fully burn the fuel, and is theoretically the perfect air/fuel ratio: it is 14.7 parts of air to 1 part of fuel. Less than that is lean, and more than that is rich. In the real world, the perfect stoichiometric ratio burns rather too hot, so making your mixture a little richer is better for the engine.

There is a quite popular theory that 'carburettor' is a French word meaning 'leave it alone'.

SU Carbs

The SU's design goes back to 1905, and is beautifully elegant and simple, as well as extremely efficient: an SU-equipped 1920s Austin Seven can achieve 50mpg plus (5.6ltr/100km). The 110-year-old principle is that as the tapered needle is withdrawn from its position blocking the jet, more fuel can be sucked into the engine. The needle is fat at the top for closed throttle openings, and it narrows down as the throttle opens, opening up the jet. The tapering shape of the needle dictates the air–fuel mixture at all throttle openings, so different needles are needed for shopping cars and for charging-around cars.

The oil and damper arrangement slows the rise of the needle to allow more fuel for acceleration, a function

SU carbs are particularly tunable, with many options of needles, jets and springs for fine control of the mixture at various rpm. It's even possible to shave your own needles in the pursuit of tuning perfection.

provided by accelerator pumps on other carb designs. Different return springs are available to tune this function. With a series of different needles and springs, you can experiment with fine-tuning SU carbs until they're exactly the way you like them. The oil for the dashpot should be lighter than engine oil, at about 10 weight.

Some people have different sets of needles and springs for track days or rallying – they can be changed in ten minutes provided you don't drop anything crucial. In fact, if you don't want to pay for serious dyno tuning, you can play about very cheaply and effectively with a private or unused section of road, a variety of different jets, needles and springs, and a stopwatch.

Weber Carbs

Weber and Dell'orto carbs are only really necessary for seriously high-performance engines that are habitually used flat out. Webers and Dell'ortos spray fuel centrally into the incoming air stream, which is ultimately

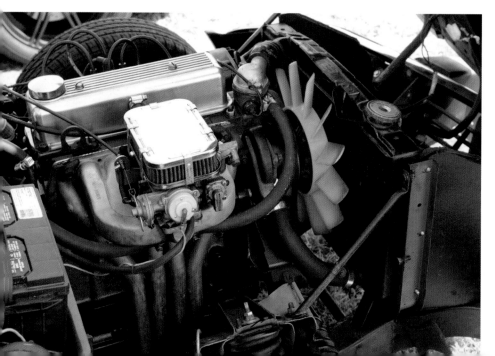

Big sidedraught Webers are normally too much for a Triumph engine, but their downdraught twin-choke or two-barrel carbs are more proportionate and are worth checking out.

a better way of doing it. But on a road engine, acceleration in the mid-range could be exactly the same with SUs or Strombergs. You might get an extra 5–10 per cent bhp flat out at peak rpm, but the cost would be worse mpg, significant initial cost, major dyno tuning time and costs, and the danger of overfuelling a small engine and wrecking it.

Webers are fun to play with, and many furiously expensive hours of fun can be had on the dyno machine pottering about with different jets, but essentially much of the work required to make a set of Webers work properly will be in reducing rather than increasing the amount of incoming fuel, to get the mixture going into the engine adjusted to something reasonable. This process rather resembles the many pointless rear disc-brake conversions carried out in the 1990s before balanced four-wheel discs became the norm on faster cars: in order to be safe to drive, rear disc conversions have to be mostly disabled to get the right 80 per cent front, 20 per cent rear braking ratio.

The last Mini I bought was a bargain because somebody had fitted a huge 40DCOE sidedraught Weber to a 1000cc engine, over-fuelling it to the extent of washing the oil off all the bores and wrecking them: the price I paid reflected the fact that the ruined engine was in the back seat of the car. Having said all that, Webers do look sexy and they do make excellent noises.

The juiciness of Webers at low rpm means that it would be wise to ensure that there's a big spark to the plugs to resist fouling.

Bike Carbs

Using Japanese bike carbs on cars is a relatively new idea. It is possible to get good results from them, but it's apparently difficult. The reason is that a bike carb relies on

Triple Mikunis on a GT6 with triple K&Ns do look cool, though I'm not sure how much fettling they need compared to SUs. V-PERFORMANCE

More Mikunis, this time on Richard Brown's competition Spitfire. Note the seriously shrouded rad and the extra sheeting keeping hot radiator air away from the carbs to avoid vaporization. V-PERFORMANCE

high gas speeds and is designed to provide a lot of fuel and air from 5,000rpm to 12,000rpm and up to 150mph (240km/h). That's emphatically not how a Triumph engine works.

Vintage Performance Developments in New York have been working with bike carbs for a while, and are very enthusiastic about the Mikuni HRS 42mm bike carbs as a direct replacement for pairs of SUs or Zeniths. They sell kits with K&N filters for just under $1,000 (www.v-performance.com).

Lucas and Modified Lucas Fuel Injection

It is still possible to find sets of Lucas PI equipment secondhand, because over the years a significant number of people have lost patience, taken them off and replaced them with a pair of carbs. There are two truths about Lucas PI: first, the pump wasn't very good, and many people have replaced it with a Bosch equivalent and are still happily injecting today. The second truth is that current pump fuel is not the same as it was in 1970, and adapting or tuning carbs to run on the stuff is easier than altering a mechanical fuel injection set-up.

It's worth mentioning that the 2500cc Triumph six was a big success in the TVR 2500 Vixen and 2500M, and almost universally their owners sooner or later converted the fuel pump to a Bosch.

One point to be made is that to work well with Lucas injection, the engine itself has to be in very good condition. If the vacuum is not 100 per cent what it's supposed to be, it can't operate the injection system properly. The same applies to sparks and timing, which also need to be spot on.

Other recommendations that have appeared regarding Lucas injection include getting a bigger alternator to ensure there's always plenty of current available to keep the pump pressure up; adding a primer pump to support the main fuel pump; and keeping the tank as full as possible to use the fuel as a heat sink to avoid vaporizing.

Fuel Vaporization

Vaporization is a problem with modern fuels in hot weather. Use a heat shield to separate the hot exhaust manifold from the carbs to avoid it, and mount the fuel pump somewhere cool if it's electric. Pouring refrigerated cold water from a vacuum flask over the outside of the carb bodies may get you started again, otherwise leave the bonnet open and take a book to read as you wait for the engine to cool down. *The Wasp Factory* by Iain Banks is recommended.

Marmite

There's probably a Marmite love-or-hate moment here: if you like the old-school simplicity and authenticity of carbs and points that can be fettled roadside, you'd probably better look away.

Modern fuel injection is much more of a practical option in 2016, as multiple coil packs, Megasquirt budget open-source computers and high-pressure fuel pumps are easily and cheaply available nowadays.

With an Electronic Fuel Injection (EFI) system, the fuel pump operates at around 60psi and carries fuel to a rail on the engine, off which are mounted fuel injectors. The computer controls when the injector fires, and can also control spark timing. It can provide more accurate fuelling and timing, can automatically retard the timing to avoid piston damage if it has a knock sensor, and can act as a rev limiter. The unused fuel is constantly recirculated to the tank, so it helps provide cool fuel and reduce vapour locks with their resultant breakdowns, bad hot starting and half-hour roadside waits with the bonnet up.

Computer control can be restricted to fuel management only, with the standard mechanical distributor and points optionally retained to keep the ignition system separate.

The more complex the system, the more it can do – crank position sensors can fire coil packs to replace the distributor, and sensors for air temperature and pressure, throttle position, exhaust oxygen levels and air/fuel mix can all be used to get more power and economy out of an engine.

The computer needs to be kept cool and not bashed about, but that applies to any electronics in a car. I once gave away a nice Scimitar with an insoluble and intolerable intermittent cutting-out problem, but found out later that the Scimitar's engine bay is just too hot for 1990s Lumenition ignition systems. That was a long while back, before I realized that just because it's new doesn't mean it works: the Lumenition system was brand new so I had discounted it as a problem.

As with alternators, many apparent problems with computers actually turn out to be problems with wires, sensors, earthing or corrosion.

Engineer Rick Patton is a Triumph enthusiast who has come up with an interesting kit that replaces the carbs on Triumph 4- and 6-cylinder engines with throttle-body injection. It's just the carb that's replaced – the air cleaner, cables and intake manifold remain the same. Although I'm not personally familiar with his system, he visibly knows what he's talking about. He uses perfectly ordinary GM injection gear, which is very available in North America (*see* www.pattonmachine.com).

I have to admit that I was mechanically KISS (keep it simple, stupid)-oriented myself until I was persuaded to write for *Fast Ford* and *Japanese Performance*, and got involved in some good sport with massively turbocharged 1,000bhp Toyota Supra engines and California dragstrip grudge matches. You can't do any of that without coming to terms with using computers for fuelling and ignition.

I like both the simple and the new-tech approaches, for different reasons. Some of my cars retain old-school technology, such as the (1974) Mini Marcos and the (1950) Bentley, which run carbs and points, albeit double points on the Bentley. The Cobra replica (probably 2018) will run with switchable petrol/propane turbo injection, which will involve a hands-on semi-DIY Megasquirt computer with two very different maps for the different fuels.

Would I use throttle body injection in a Triumph? Well, I wouldn't use it on the Midge because it looks like a pre-war special. Six Amal bike carbs would be cool, though.

With a Spitfire or a GT6, the answer would actually depend on the current condition of the distributor and carbs in front of me. If everything was fine I would leave it alone. If I found that I needed to spend money and time on rebuilding the carbs and distributor anyway, I might well go for throttle body injection and a Megasquirt computer instead. The modern control systems can offer minor but worthwhile gains in power and in fuel economy.

A distributor does pretty well in providing a spark at the right time, and the mechanical bobweights in the distributor do a good job of advancing the spark to an appropriate place for good power. However, any wear in bearings and the erosion of sparking faces on points,

Triple Strombergs on a 2500cc TR6 engine? No, count the fuel tubes – this is a set of injection throttle bodies from PattonMachine. They still look like Strombergs, but generate significantly more power. PATTONMACHINE

combined with the variable quality of new aftermarket replacements for old Lucas parts, means that most traditionally fuelled and sparked Triumph engines don't run at peak power and efficiency for very long.

Air Filters

K&N claim that their oiled cotton filters increase airflow by a massive percentage, and they're right. Some standard air filters can be quite restrictive. If you're looking for serious performance, using a good quality, free-flow air filter to replace a standard and potentially restrictive tin box with a couple of little intake pipes is sensible. However, the original standard filters, kept fresh, work fine for street use and mildly modified engines.

Ramjets

Ramjets, or ram pipes or trumpets, are not really ramjets at all. They neither ram nor jet anything, but they are effective gasflow smoothers. Any sharp angles in gas paths should be avoided, and that includes the edges of carbs that are not fitted with trumpets. So ram pipes or velocity stacks that smooth the path of incoming air into the mouth of the carb are well worthwhile.

IGNITION

Distributors

If you find a Delco distributor on your engine, and you have notions of improving your car's performance, put it in the spares box in the boot and buy a Lucas distributor instead. The advance curve of the Delco is just not suitable for performance, and nor is its advance curve as easily modified as the Lucas.

The cost of replacing the minor wearing parts of a standard Triumph ignition system is about the same as a pizza. Do it annually, and keep the old kit in a box in the boot.

If all goes well, electric current generates a magnetic field in the coil, which is discharged via the contact points and condenser to the spark plugs. This happens about 150 times per second.

The condenser reduces the power of the spark at the points, and slows their erosion.

The timing of the spark needs to be quite accurate, and its accuracy is affected by the condition of the shaft and bearings of the distributor.

A vacuum advance system alters the timing; advancing it as high vacuum is generated by wide throttle openings and rising revs. Distributors can have different advance curves to sharpen performance.

from an LED through to a photo-electric switch that acts as a trigger and sends current to the spark plug. This cuts out the spark-based erosion of the surface of the points, and is less sensitive to wear in the distributor shaft and bearings.

There are various systems available, the newer of which are entirely contained within the standard distributor and cap. If you use an electronic ignition system with an external box, make sure it doesn't get too hot – some of them fail if overheated. It's worth using good quality kit for ignition – a 200bhp engine can lose 100bhp if the ignition is duff.

Use colder plugs for hotter engines, as hot plugs can pre-ignite. Pre-ignition is similar to detonation, and it means a mistimed explosion in the combustion chamber rather than a controlled burn. It's almost as destructive to bearings and pistons as detonation – though your ruined piston won't care about which one destroyed it.

Fresh plug leads are a good idea, and replacing old ones with fat and expensive 7mm or 8mm plug leads will guarantee no loss of power to the spark.

For high-compression engines using high revs, a fat spark is important, so when replacing the ignition coil uprate it to a more powerful alternative such as an Aldon Flamethower. MSD ignition can be had with a rev limiter and cockpit-adjustable timing, which would be nice.

Electronics

Megaspark is an open source DIY computer for timing with the distributor retained. You can certainly tackle the ignition first and then the fuelling later, although fuelling does need to be injection to be properly controlled – there are options with computer-controlled carbs but they are a nightmare and are now rare.

Whether you want to get involved with computers and dealing with sensors for exhaust gas temperature, timing, air–fuel mixture, load, throttle position, oxygen, catalytic convertors and the rest, depends almost entirely on whether you would regard the whole process as an interesting challenge or a confounded nuisance. Ultimately, your Triumph can run just fine on carbs and points, although it would be slightly more fuel-efficient and/or powerful with computer control. For a weekend car, there's no substantial difference other than flavour.

123ignition in Holland have an interesting option: an electronic distributor that replaces the Lucas unit used in Triumphs, MGBs and Minis. It offers vacuum advance, automatic dwell, spark balancing, automatic power cut to the coil after one second, spark retardation while changing

Distributors need to be in excellent condition to maintain accurate spark timing, and the bobweights need to be clean and lubricated to get the most out of the rest of the engine. Optical points remove the need for regular points replacement and adjustment.

Points wear out and need adjustment, and they also bounce at high rpm, so optical points offer a useful and externally invisible improvement.

For a basic setting, you're looking for a static timing setting of 13 degrees BTDC – Before (the piston reaches) Top Dead Centre. Free off and lubricate the bobweights under the plate that mounts the contact points, but don't overdo the oiling. Weaker bobweight springs allow a faster advance for more extreme engines.

If the engine starts pinking or detonating, the ignition is too advanced and must be retarded until that stops, because it damages the pistons.

Optical breakerless points use a 'chopper', which is a circular plate with slots cut in it. The slots allow a light beam gear, and other bonuses. One option is a set of sixteen different advance curves chosen via a little switch. Getting the advance curve right could get you more power than an extra carb. The drive for a mechanical tachometer is missing, but Smiths, www.jdo1.com and www.casu.nl can now rebuild their old tachos to read an electric signal. There's also a more sophisticated option that can be tuned on a laptop. UK dealers are Minispares and the MG Owners' Club.

As ever, keep the old distributor in the spares box in the boot in case there is a failure of any electronic replacement: this can happen to anyone.

Forced Induction: Superchargers and Turbochargers

Sometimes, and apparently amazingly, pristine and almost unused 1950s and 1960s superchargers are discovered under benches in suburban garages, still in their original packaging. There is actually a very good reason for this, which is that some of them were almost completely useless. They were fitted briefly to people's cars, then taken back off and shoved under a bench until somebody a couple of generations younger finds them and does the same thing again.

Modern superchargers work rather better, though.

There is a conceptual and structural difference between turbochargers and superchargers. Superchargers are rather old-school and use engine power, usually provided by a belt drive, to compress air and fuel and force them into the engine under pressure, which gets more mixture in and results in a bigger bang and more power. A turbocharger uses waste gas pressure in the exhaust system to spin up a compressor at much higher speeds in order to jam a lot more mixture in.

Superchargers are constantly boosting at usually a lower pressure, but they are beneficial in that they apply smooth and continuous pressure to the engine components, which almost stops the wear created by engine braking exacerbating any slop in bearings as power comes on and off.

A turbocharger makes no parasitic demand on the engine at low revs, and while it doesn't really have any effect on the engine at low revs, it pushes in a lot of power quite suddenly when it gets up to speed. The delay before the turbocharger spools up to speed is known as turbo lag and is potentially dangerous when combined with dodgy suspension geometry such as swing axles.

The reason the 1990s Subaru Impreza Turbo feels so wickedly fast is that it has a very low final drive ratio, so cruising revs are high and the turbo is constantly almost on boost: acceleration is instant although fuel economy is relatively poor.

The supercharger is a mechanical pump limited by its speed and capacity, but a turbo uses waste exhaust gas and has huge potential power: it must be limited by blow-off valves and waste-gates. The maximum turbo pressure you can use on street petrol is about 13lb in brief pulls, although one interesting idea I'm playing with at the moment is a propane turbocharged replica Cobra, which will use 4.6-litre quad-cam V8 Mustang mechanicals and propane-fuelled turbocharging. Propane has an octane rating of 110 or so, which is equivalent to race fuel, and enters the engine very cold, which allows insane boost pressures without pistons melting. From a 4600cc engine with 34lb of boost, I could – briefly – achieve more than 600bhp.

It is interesting to wonder if that engine could be crammed into a Spitfire, although the Triumph diff internals would turn to shiny mince before the car even moved. A Jag axle would handle it, with no bother. Unfortunately there is not really enough room in a small Triumph for both petrol and propane tanks, but a dedicated turbocharged gas-fuelled engine could run insane boost and would also cost half as much to run as a petrol-fed engine, as propane/LPG is much cheaper than petrol.

Coming back to the normal world, the sensible supercharging of a Triumph engine would be a period-suitable, sympathetic, effective and unboltable modification. There's a rather glorious precedent, too: Supermarine Spitfires' Merlin engines were also supercharged.

What's Going to Break Next?

I was involved a while back with a Toyota Supra turbocharged to approaching 1,000bhp, with one huge turbo and mostly driven on race fuel to avoid piston melt, and it was almost impossible to keep the tyres from burning out on take-off. The evil beast rarely went more than a few weeks without blowing a gearbox, diff or unbreakable carbon propshaft. That principle is universal: once the engine is seriously stronger, the next weakest link in the drivetrain will break – clutch, gearbox, diff, shafts, U/Js. Frequently the gearbox lets go first. The Triumph drivetrain would really need to be entirely replaced before any serious power could be applied. I would have to admit that we are now getting well out of the milieu of 'everyday modifications'.

Given the relative fragility of the Triumph drivetrain, turbocharging would probably be unwise – the hooligan lurks within us all. However, given the above, you could

This was a new electronic distributor with optical points, which worked very well until it packed up and stranded me. If I'd kept the old points distributor in the boot, I could have driven home rather than being towed.

run a small supercharger for some useful extra grunt, and they do make a pleasing noise and are in period for the cars. Just 5lb or 6lb of supercharger pressure could get you an extra 30 per cent of power. Through a standard gearbox and diff, you would need to feed the power in smoothly, but you could definitely use it. When a 5-litre Ford 302 V8 is fitted to a TR6, all the power – 240 or so bhp – can be used, provided that it's applied smoothly. If you get rough with it, the differential will let go fairly quickly.

ENGINE BAY ELECTRICS

We've mentioned upgrading to an alternator, but quite a few of us will have had an engine inexplicably fail to start after refitting it, only to realize that we'd forgotten to attach the earth strap. Most Triumph earth straps are elderly, dirty and frayed, and it's worth upgrading to bigger and fatter wire with clean contacts. The same applies to the main cable to the starter.

Reducing current loads through elderly wires and between geriatric components is an excellent idea, and it can be achieved by adding relays into circuits. On many old Triumphs, the headlight switch takes the full current load and acts as a slow-blow fuse. Better and brighter headlights are available, but they use even more current: without a relay, darkness looms.

It is worth changing to a new modern fusebox with modern blade fuses, as they are available everywhere, unlike old-school fuses, which are as hard to find as furniture that's not made out of congealed porridge. Alternatively, buy many glass fuses when you get the chance, and add them to the box of old points and condensers in the boot.

Wire ends should be neatly cut, twisted and soldered, and freshly crimped connections should be pulled fairly hard to make sure they're sound. While old bullet connectors on the end of wires can be cleaned up and successfully reused, that's less likely with the connecting female fittings inside the rubber or plastic tubes. Throw them away and buy new ones.

Dielectric grease in all contacts will delay corrosion and faults.

ALTERNATIVE ENGINES

It's debatable whether upgrading to a completely different, sensible-sized, alternative 4-cylinder engine comes within the sphere of everyday modifications, but more and more people are fitting modern or semi-modern Japanese engines to Spitfires, so we'll include them here.

For a change from a Triumph engine to a similar 4-cylinder modern engine, you will have to deal with the following:

- Making or modifying engine mounts
- Making or modifying gearbox mounts
- Connecting combinations of different bores of cooling hoses and heater hoses to different locations
- Having a hybrid custom propshaft made and balanced
- Converting from or to hydraulic clutch operation
- Designing a smooth run and making mounts for a custom throttle cable
- Adapting a choke cable
- Concocting or adapting an exhaust manifold that clears chassis beams, and either connecting to or replacing the exhaust system
- Electrical connections for ignition, fuel pump, tachometer, oil-pressure gauge and warning light, temperature gauge, voltmeter
- Conversion from dynamo to alternator: probably easier than adapting a newer engine to run on a dynamo, and modern engines may not run if there is not enough battery/alternator power available
- For injected engines, there needs to be a return fuel line from the fuel tank to the engine
- Many later engines have no distributor, and run on coil packs and a fuel and ignition computer

Is this some new Triumph engine we've never heard of? No, it's a VVC K-series MG engine with a Triumph badge stuck on it. Light, powerful and reliable once sorted, it's not a bad choice for a Spit. The Spitfire 1500 engine is an MG Midget engine as well, so there is a precedent.

♦ Dealing with a gear lever that erupts in a different place, and transmission tunnel adaptation (easy with cardboard Triumph transmission tunnels)

♦ For any serious additional power, stiffening the structure of the car and improving the brakes and suspension

Sports Six Club Uprated Engines

At the time of writing, the Triumph Sports Six Club (TSSC) offers a range of exchange engines. Rebuilt standard-spec engines for Heralds and Spitfires are £1,840, and that rises to what sounds like a seriously nice high-performance 6-cylinder engine at £3,275: the spec includes a polished and ported head with special valves, a dual timing chain, a lightened flywheel, a Nitrided crank, and the whole rotating assembly balanced.

Joining the TSSC is strongly recommended anyway.

The Toyota 4AGE engine comes in many variations and is popular with the kit-car community, which is always a good sign. Kit-car builders can use any engine they want, so their choices can be illuminating. Fitting something like the 4AGE Toyota engine with a five-speed box and running it on carbs is a sensible upgrade that will improve the performance and reliability of a Spitfire without substantially changing its character. The 4AGE engine is a 1600cc, oversquare, short-stroke, high-revving design with a twin-cam head as an option, and it offers, in standard form, power levels from 80bhp to 135bhp with usually at least 100lb ft of torque. Its red line goes up to 7,600rpm depending on the model. It still has a distributor and can be run with carbs, so it's not far in spirit from the original engine – it's a sensible ex-saloon-car motor ideal for upgrading a light sports car.

The Maxda MX5/Miata drivetrain is also well worth thinking about, as it is extremely and cheaply available, and offers 1600cc and 1800cc twin-cam engines of 110–135bhp. You do have to deal with injection and computers, as there's no distributor and the plugs are fired by coil packs and an ECU. You can also use the Mazda's seats, which are very good.

On the positive side of modern Japanese engines, any 1800 Mazda drivetrain bought for a few hundred pounds out of a gently crashed MX5 will deliver horsepower that a Triumph engine can't deliver without thousands of pounds' worth of serious engineering and probably a supercharger. It also comes with a free overdrive fifth gear and a much stronger gearbox, and will probably last for 200,000 miles (320,000km), no bother.

If you're looking for an engineering challenge, though, and you would enjoy the process of using a drill and grinding stone to work on the ports of a Triumph engine to achieve more horsepower with your own hands, simply substituting a 4AGE wouldn't be much fun at all. To change a Triumph for a Toyota 4AGE, you need to make engine and gearbox mounts, get a hybrid propshaft made and balanced, connect the exhaust system to a slightly different manifold, organize coolant and heater hoses to possibly a larger radiator, adjust the engine wiring locations, adapt

The slant 16-valve four from the Triumph Dolomite has been used in Spitfires: the 2000cc Sprint version achieved 125bhp and came with a large, strong gearbox, but had head gasket issues.

throttle and choke linkages, make or modify a transmission tunnel cover, adapt your clutch pedal to a cable linkage, and tell your insurance company what you've been up to. Having done that lot, though, you probably won't have any more mechanical work to do, ever, apart from the suspension and the back axle.

You might well have doubled the horsepower of your Spitfire, and that can have consequences. Untamed transverse-leaf back suspension with swing axles is a much worse problem on a fast car.

There can be unexpected consequences with dramatic powerplant changes, partly to do with the engineering dictum that every change generates ten other unexpected changes. I encountered massive, boring and irrelevant mechanical problems myself with early 4.2-litre XJ6 engines, gearboxes and the overdrive in the Ayrspeed XK120 replica production prototype, which were nothing to do with my chassis and body designs or the redesigned and narrowed rear suspension: my mechanicals just happened to come from a period of very bad Jaguar quality control. I ran out of patience, threw the third engine and second gearbox in a skip and replaced it with a Rover V8 and a five-speed. This was a huge dynamic improvement, as the car then started instantly, changed gear whenever I asked it, and the main bearings lasted a lot more than 1,000 miles (1,600km). There was a downside, though – the car may have been dramatically improved, but it was no longer a Jag, and had definitely lost its original flavour. Perhaps I should have found an earlier 3.8-litre XK engine or a later 4-litre AJ6 Jag engine, matched with a T5 five-speed. That would have been reliable but would still

have retained the massive heft and mass, and the smooth baritone growl of a Jag straight six. I was supposed to be prototyping the chassis concept, though, not wasting time on engines.

Perhaps the lesson to learn from my experience is that if you like the flavour of a Triumph, look for an engine that doesn't change the character of the car too much. Maybe a Spitfire just needs a more powerful and advanced 1300cc–1600cc 4-cylinder engine that comes with a five-speed box. Having said that, a Spit 6 – a GT6 mongrel with an open Spitfire body – will always be a delight.

If you're thinking about a dramatic engine change, be sure you're going to love the result before throwing serious money and time at the project. Even a simple change to a similar alternative engine gets complicated: you would have to enjoy that challenge as well as the results. Track down someone who's done the conversion you're thinking about, and ask for a ride: nobody will turn down the chance to show off their pride and joy.

If you think contaminating fine period British workmanship with a modern Japanese or German engine is sacrilege and spoils the car, that's also a valid point of view. A well tuned, pre-1973, 1300 Spitfire can be a great deal of fun, and although the 1300 is never going to be as powerful or as reliable as a modern Japanese four, it's by no means a bad engine.

Silly Alternative Engines

The Americans, inelegantly but perspicaciously, say that there 'ain't no substitoot for cubes'. This has some truth

The 2500cc version of the Triumph six was used in the 1970s TVR 2500M, a thoroughly nice car: it weighed the same as a TR6 so performance was similar.

to it. If you put a 5-litre engine where there used to be a 2-litre engine, your car will go very fast indeed and will be a great deal more fun to drive, although terrifying if unsorted.

You then have to improve the drivetrain and rear axle, and the suspension and the brakes. And probably the chassis as well. However, a V8 Spitfire conversion isn't really an 'everyday modification', and it would be wise to warn your insurance broker to put on some incontinence pants before even asking for a quote for a 5-litre Spitfire.

Food for thought – a veritable banquet for thought, in fact – is engine weight. The Triumph 2-litre all-iron straight six weighs 460lb (209kg) while the thin-crankcase-walled Ford 5-litre 302CI V8 weighs 475lb (215kg) – the Chevy 350CI V8 is 525lb (238kg). But an aluminium 3500cc (or 4600cc) Rover V8 weighs just 355lb (161kg). So a Spit Rover would have excellent balance.

The Death Rattle

The 'death rattle' on starting a cold Triumph engine makes most people wince, but it's not as bad as it sounds, and the six can carry on for many years even if it sounds like a diesel with the big ends gone when you start it up. What's happening is that the oil has drained out of the original oil filter back into the sump, and it's a good few seconds before there is any oil pressure. On my own Vitesse Midge, I've retained the original mechanical fuel pump as well as the oil filter, so by the time the fuel has been pumped up to the carbs and the engine finally starts, there's already oil pressure in the bearings, so all is well. Changing to a remote oil filter avoids the problem, and the later spin-on filters work better anyway.

Crankshaft end float is the other routine bogey with Triumph sixes. The 'death sentence' used to be applied to

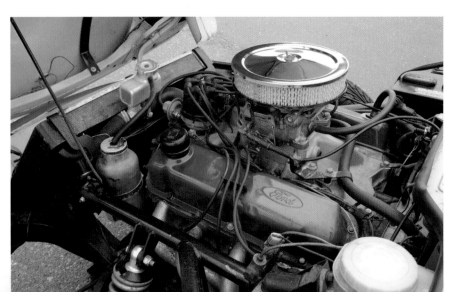

Now we're definitely getting away from everyday modifications, but it was a surprise to find that a GT6 with a 5-litre Ford V8 handled and balanced very well indeed.

The Ford V8 does require some gentle massaging of the Triumph body and chassis, but these mods stiffened the GT6 strongly enough for several years of hard use, with no cracks appearing to date.

sixes with too much crankshaft end float, but that sentence can now be commuted to a repair in some cases. Sometimes the end float can be shimmed out with larger crank shims, which can be fitted via the sump without removing the engine. Racetorations now offer a service involving machining and an additional thrust washer, which has had to be developed as there isn't an endless supply of good cylinder blocks, and many have previously been scrapped because of this problem. The way to check for crankshaft end float is to get someone to operate the clutch or to pull hard on the front pulley, and see how far the crankshaft moves forwards.

When cleaning out the sump, you may well find a plug in the bottom of it. This comes from the rocker shaft, and needs to be put back in place and secured with Loctite or similar.

The Triumph 4- and 6-cylinder engines fitted to Heralds, Vitesses, Spitfires, GT6s and 6-cylinder TRs have a long history going back to the 4-cylinder Standard 8 of 1953. The engine started off producing 28bhp, and ended up making 150bhp in its final injected 6-cylinder 2500cc form.
R. HAWKINS

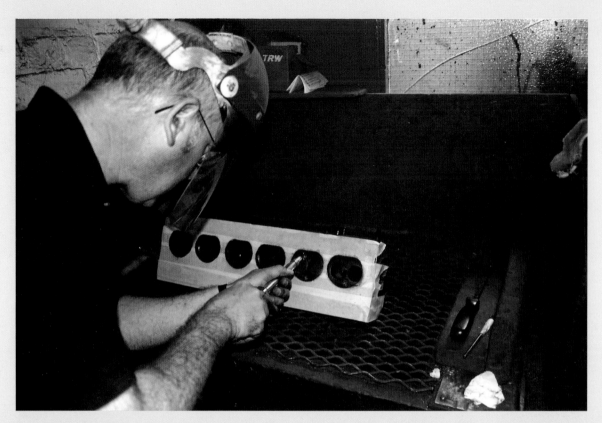

The author, porting and polishing his own Triumph cylinder head. The masking tape is to avoid scratching the face of the head if the grinder slips.

This is the valve seat that will be milled out and will end up on the workshop floor, so it doesn't matter how long you stall before tackling the job.

The old valve seat and the area surrounding it is milled out.

As you can see, the whole seat area is gone: the hardened valve seat ring is quite large.

The new ring is frozen while the cylinder head is heated, so the new seat is well jammed in place. They rarely fall out once fitted.

The new seats have now been treated to some gasflow engineering – the idea is to provide a smooth and open entry into and out of the cylinder as well as allowing the valves to seal perfectly.

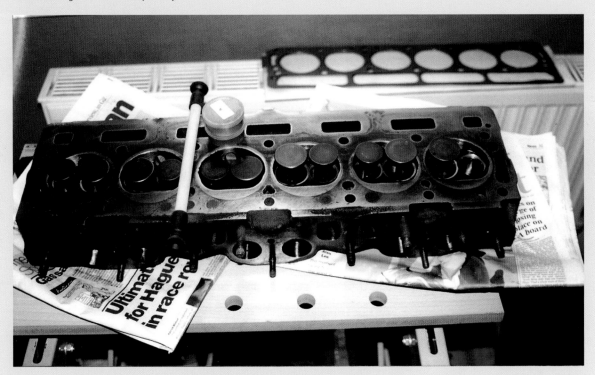

4

transmission

HORRIBLE NOISES

There are a good few horrible noises produced by the smaller Triumph gearboxes that will convince you of the imminent disintegration of your drivetrain, but one or two of them are to some extent false alarms. A disintegrating cardboard gearbox tunnel sounds just like a disintegrating gearbox. New ones are now either fibreglass or plastic, both of which are a structural improvement, but both allow a lot more noise into the cabin unless lined with firmly attached noise insulation material.

Old Rotoflex drive couplings also make some very unpleasant noises while in the process of collapsing. They are a wearing part and need to be replaced now and again. Check them for cracking through stress or old age.

In the end, genuine and terminal horrible noises are sadly a fact of life with Triumph gearboxes. Low-powered Heralds driven by old ladies might manage rather more, but a Triumph gearbox is generally going to require a

rebuild at 50,000 miles (80,450km) if driven gently, and at about 20,000 miles (32,000km) if it's driven hard.

If you want to stick with four speeds and a Triumph box, it may help to know that the Mk IV Spitfire's all-synchro box is based on the stronger GT6 gearbox, as is the Marina box. Be that as it may, sooner or later your Triumph is going to provide you with the opportunity to upgrade its gearbox.

FIVE GEARS OR SIX?

Before committing to either a five-speed gearbox conversion or the addition of an overdrive on third and fourth gears to total six gears, the fun-per-quid ratio has to be calculated. If you don't drive fast and far, you may not get much at all out of the additional gear or gears. All you're really doing is dropping the rpm while cruising, which reduces noise, improves mpg slightly and reduces engine wear slightly. If you're only going to be driving in the UK and prefer A-roads to motorways, the ever-increasing

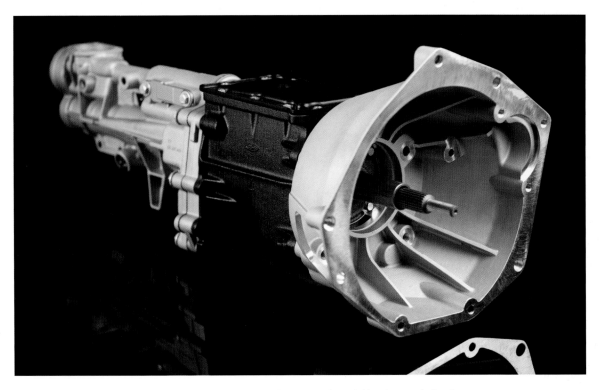

The Sierra-sourced Ford box has a rather low first gear, but there are better internals available to improve the box for sports-car use.

road crowding means you may not get to use an over-drive much anyway. MP Greg Hands has said that rather than the official figure of 60,000,000 for the UK population, Tesco estimates it to be 80,000,000 based on grocery sales, and many new immigrants don't buy food at Tesco. Also, the annual population increase is between 500,000 and 1,000,000. So depending on where you are in the increasingly crowded and slowing road network, an addi-tional gear may get so little use in future as to be a waste of money. However, you should still demand money off when buying four-geared cars due to their unsuitability for modern conditions – and let's hope the seller hasn't read this book.

Look carefully at the overdrive cost/benefit analysis, adding into it the detail that a converted-to-overdrive car is not necessarily worth much more than a four-speed, although it will probably be easier to sell. I personally am increasingly feeling the need for a TR6, and the next book in this series might be on TRs, which would provide an excellent reason/excuse to buy one. I live in a spacious land with no speed cameras, so I would be actively look-ing for a TR6 with overdrive, and I might not bother look-ing at four-speeds unless I get an excellent price that will allow funding for a five-speed conversion. You won't get much of your money back on a conversion as such, but you might well add to the equation a fast sale at a good price, which is well worth thinking about.

Another factor again is that the smaller Triumph gear-box simply isn't very strong, and just wears out; in par-ticular this applies to the 6-cylinder Triumphs up to 2 litres. Even if you weren't bothered about the extra gear, a Ford five-speed will last a lot longer than a small Triumph gearbox, and is cheap to rebuild or replace even if you do manage to wear it out. Normally, a competently over-hauled Ford box would outlive the car. The gear-shifting can be baulky and awkward on the Type 9 Ford box, but this can be both repaired and improved with a quickshift kit.

Ford's intention seems to have been that the gearbox would never be drained, and that its initial oil-fill would last the life of the car, but obviously carrying out occa-sional gearbox oil changes is a better idea than not doing so. BGH Geartech have a good reputation and much expertise in the internals of these gearboxes. Talk to them about the best Ford box to look for: the standard Sierra box has ratios suited to a heavy saloon, with a low first and second gear, so you might want to think about a close-ratio gear set if you're going for a rebuild anyway.

Access to the Triumph gearboxes is very good, as the transmission tunnel is detachable. This remote is being extended for kit-car use, but it could equally easily be shortened if you moved a 6-cylinder engine back in a Triumph chassis for better balance.

Dynamically, a typical Ford Type 9 conversion will have similar fifth-speed gearing to the overdrive fourth gearing on a Triumph box, and is simply a conventional gearbox with five speeds.

An overdrive isn't quite the same – it is an additional two-speed gearbox with its own internal clutch, fitted behind the original four-speed Triumph gearbox. It operates on third and fourth gears and gives you more ratios to play with, although overdrive third feels similar to normal fourth. The overdrive slides in with its own clutch, and although you can just flick it in and out using that internal clutch, you would normally back off the throttle after flicking the switch, to make the change smoother and to preserve the clutch. I personally tend to dip the main clutch as well when going in and out of overdrive, making life very easy indeed for the overdrive unit. I've only needed one rebuild on my Vitesse overdrive unit, in about 1985.

The gear ratios of a Spitfire 1500 with overdrive, as compared to the Ford gearbox from a 1.6/2.0 Pinto (Sierra), are as follows:

Triumph: O/D fourth 0.797:1; fourth 1:1; third 1.11:1; second 1.39:1; first 2.16:1

Ford: Fifth 0.82:1; fourth 1:1; third 1.37; second 1.97; first 3.65:1

On a Triumph with a smaller and less powerful engine, you might not have enough torque to get much use out of an overdrive. An engine at low revs produces a lower percentage of its available power, and a small engine may need to cruise at higher rpm to provide enough power to get up hills. I run a very high final drive ratio on my daily driver car, which is a beaten-up old 1958 Chevy Delray with later mechanicals: I can do that because I have 300lb ft of torque. The car has a GM overdrive 700R4 automatic, and I recently had the rear axle rebuilt with a new differential and the final drive ratio changed from 3.55:1 to 3.08:1 to give it even longer legs. I've effectively added an overdrive gear to the overdrive.

However, that is on a 5.7-litre V8 engine with massive torque in a relatively light although large 3,500lb (1,590kg) car, and I can drive it up mountains with no bother, even with that gearing. With a small engine, you might have to change down a gear or come out of overdrive to go up a gentle slope on a motorway. A 6-cylinder Triumph will get more out of an overdrive; on a 4-cylinder, it's perhaps something of a luxury. Join a Triumph club and have a ride in a small-engined overdrive car before you pay out big money for a conversion. *Triumph World* editor Simon Goldsworthy disagrees on this, and feels that an overdrive is a real bonus on any Triumph: he would be unlikely to buy a Vitesse, Spitfire or GT6 without overdrive. He has driven many more Triumphs than I have, so his view carries a lot of weight.

Another option to a gearbox change is to alter the final drive ratio in the differential. The Herald's standard 4.11:1 is pretty low for today's traffic and allows a cruising speed of 60mph (100km/h) or so, which is actually borderline dangerous when average motorway speeds are more than 80mph (130km/h) and foreign trucks either don't know the speed limits or don't care. Mind you, speed cameras are now appearing on UK motorways, so with that and the monthly increase in general crowding, the average motorway speed will soon come down to an indicated 70mph (110km/h), which is about 65mph (105km/h) allowing for speedo 'error'. (GPS gives your actual speed: speedos read over by around 10 per cent.)

Lowering the final drive ratio to a 3.89:1 diff would raise your comfortable cruising speed, but at the expense of slower acceleration from a standstill. It's worth noting that the Herald was a family car, originally geared to carry four passengers and luggage up hills. Nowadays it is usually only required to carry two people and a picnic basket, in which case it can use a higher-geared rear axle with ease.

Toyota Supra and Celica boxes offer good quality and smooth actions, and the six-speed R380 box in later Land Rovers is an interesting option. The T5 as fitted to 302 V8 Mustangs is a very good bit of kit that can handle anything any Triumph engine can throw at it.

RETRO-FITTING OVERDRIVES

If you can find an overdrive unit rescued from an overdrive-equipped car to fit to a non-overdrive car, that's an excellent idea, with a few provisos.

If you're raiding an existing car, ideally you will need to collect the overdrive unit, the gearbox mounting plate and the mounting, a shorter or shortened propshaft, an angle drive for the speedo cable, the column-mounted or gear lever-mounted switch and the wiring, with a relay for the J-type overdrive. Unless you've driven the donor car with the overdrive unit in it and know that the mechanical operation is good and the clutch is all right, it's going to be worth having the overdrive unit checked over and serviced.

The wiring isn't a big deal, although faulty wiring is a very frequent reason for overdrive malfunctions. First it requires power, preferably from the switched side of the ignition, as you don't need it to be powered unless the engine is running. Then it needs the lockout wiring, which prevents it from destructively engaging while you're in reverse, first or second gears. Finally it needs to be earthed.

Clutch operation is hydraulic, so release bearings of the annular type mounted inside the bellhousing can be used with different gearboxes. It's always the inaccessible parts that go wrong, but removing a Triumph gearbox is relatively easy.

The secondhand overdrive options currently available were both made by Laycock, and are either the D-type from earlier Spitfires, or the J-type from Dolomites and later Spitfires, which also have synchromesh on first gear. The Dolomite Sprint/Triumph 2000 gearboxes don't fit, and changing a 4-cylinder to the Vitesse/GT6 box is more trouble than it's worth.

The J-type will need the right clutch and flywheel, and the later all-synchro box has bigger flywheel bolts. They can still be used, but they need bushes made. You can't use the Dolomite flywheel as it uses a different later starter motor. The front and the back flanges of the propshaft need to match the diff and the gearbox: there are larger and smaller options.

It used to be possible to change the overdrive ratio from the usual 22.5 per cent reduction to 28 per cent, giving a much higher final drive ratio and low rpm cruising – if you're having an overdrive rebuilt, that would be the time to talk to the shop about the possibility of finding the necessary parts, which would almost certainly be second-hand. You would only want to do that on a six, though.

Don't discard the gearbox that you took out to replace with an overdrive box – being able to return the car to its original condition might be valuable later.

OVERDRIVE REPAIRS

Most overdrive failures and foul-ups are caused by wiring. This is similar to what alternator reconditioning companies find very frequently – when they test a 'failed' alternator handed in as a core for exchange, there's very often (about 60 per cent of the time) nothing wrong with it at all: it was a fault in the car's wiring that caused the problem. The same applies to overdrive wiring, which in addition is under the car and attacked by rain and salt.

The circuit for the overdrive is fairly simple: power goes through the switch to the overdrive unit, and then to earth. With the ignition on and the gearbox in third or fourth, check that there is power in the circuit as far as the relay and then the solenoid, and that the overdrive itself is earthed. The solenoid can also require adjustment and possibly replacement.

It is possible to completely strip an overdrive unit on a DIY basis, although it's quite complex. It would be worth changing the oil and having a look at what comes out. I have been warned not to turn either a gearbox or an overdrive unit upside down unless it is about to be fully stripped. This is because fifty years of steel swarf, particles and bits of old layshaft, which have previously been sitting harmlessly in the bottom, are upended all over the internal components and bearings. That warning does make sense.

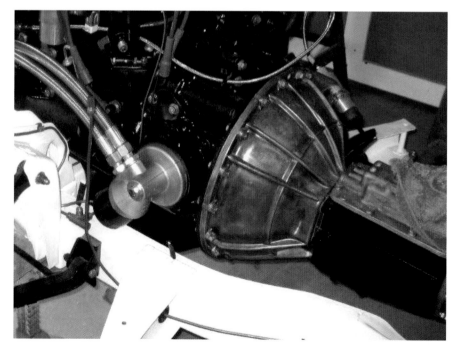

The Standard- and then Herald-derived gearbox on the GT6 is physically quite small, so there's no real option for uprating it with bigger bearings and gears.
R. LAMBRECHT

GEARBOX REPAIRS

If you're getting a box rebuilt, get an uprated laygear set if possible. Layshaft hardening is an important part of the manufacturing process and there are no more OEM parts. Any new parts made have no Triumph quality control, and therefore are all now automatically suspect as far as quality goes. The shafts are made of ordinary steel to retain ductility, but although the outside is supposed to be case-hardened, the quality of modern parts has to be checked. Bang a new layshaft with an old one to see if it's hard enough. If the new one bruises, send it back and demand a harder one. That's the budget way of doing it: you can also ask a machine shop to test it against the Rockwell scale for specific adequate hardness.

You might be tempted to indulge in a set of straight-cut close-ratio gears, which are stronger than standard. They're quite noisy, although the noise they make is redolent of period racetracks and will please all such enthusiasts – but for a road car it's something you should be sure to experience at first hand before getting your credit card out.

It may not be super successful to mix and match bits of several old gearboxes, as you're combining many different sorts, extents and directions of wear. The wear might accelerate when worn parts are introduced to other worn parts. However, you might be lucky and get another couple of years out of an amalgamated collection of the least bad bits of several gearboxes. It helps that the Triumph gearboxes can be taken out of the cars from the inside, saving a great deal of inverted grovelling with oily grit getting in your eyes, as happens with lesser cars – so if you would enjoy the process and the challenge, carry on!

It's worth reflecting that professional gearbox rebuilders face the same shortage of parts, so it's reasonable to give them some slack as far as supplying you with a perfect and silent gearbox goes. Prices will also rise as available secondhand parts evaporate. Having said that, if a pro shop has rebuilt your box and it jumps out of second, it's still their problem rather than yours.

THE TR6 OPTION

It has to be faced that the gearboxes fitted to the small Triumphs up to Vitesse and GT6 aren't really up to the job. Heralds and Spitfires driven gently will last reasonably well, but enthusiastic use will involve failures and rebuilds. A 6-cylinder engine given any exercise will soon result in the small gearbox getting tired and emotional, and a tuned six will have a gearbox giving up fairly quickly.

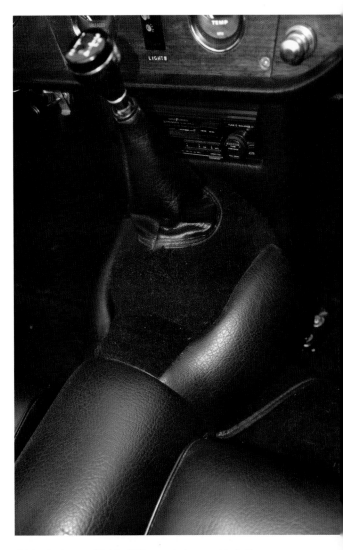

This is what a normal Spitfire/GT6 transmission tunnel looks like. Alteration is easy, as the tunnel is made of either cardboard, plastic or GRP.

One relatively expensive but likely permanent solution to the problem is to replace the smaller gearbox with a bigger and preferably overdrive box from a TR6. This lasts well in a fairly powerful and heavy TR6, which weighs a ballpark 2,500lb (1,135kg) as compared to the Spitfire's ballpark 1,600lb (725kg).

When you've tracked down a TR6 gearbox, that begs the question as to whether you should consider upgrading to the TR6 engine that might also be available: you might well be looking at the remains of a rust-scrapped TR6 as a source of parts.

A new transmission tunnel has been created inside this GT6 cabin to accommodate the larger TR6 gearbox. It all works, but it's pretty tight.

The answer is that the TR6 uses the same cylinder block as the 2-litre Vitesse and the GT6: the additional 500cc of cylinder capacity of the TR6 was achieved by increasing the stroke. So you can successfully improve both the gearbox and the torque and bhp numbers of a Vitesse, GT6 or Spit 6 as well as its gearbox reliability, by fitting a TR6 engine and box. The sump is different between TR6 and GT6/Vitesse engines, and you will need to use a 2-litre sump and modify (bash out) the bottom of the sump to provide clearance for the longer throws of the 2.5-litre crankshaft.

Possibly useful information is that the Stag uses the same gearbox as the TR6. This might just be mildly interesting and only marginally relevant, but just about every blown-up Stag converted to a Rover V8 will have used the gearbox that came with the Rover engine – so there might be a good few nice Stag gearboxes still gathering rust under garage benches. The Stag box is apparently good for up to 160bhp.

The TR6 gearbox is significantly physically bigger than the Herald-based box, but fortunately from a conversion point of view, the transmission tunnel is made of cardboard rather than steel, and there are new transmission tunnels available in both plastic and fibreglass that can be relatively easily adapted, although they need padding to reduce mechanical noise.

The big TR6 gearbox fits reasonably well between the smaller cars' chassis rails, after some adjustment with a grinder: this one is in a GT6. It doesn't fit inside the normal transmission tunnel, though.

The chassis will also have to be modified for clearance to get the TR6 gearbox between the rails, which is going to be less easy than enlarging the tunnel, but is unavoidable.

CLUTCHES

Don't ride the clutch, on the 6-cylinder cars in particular. This is what causes the crank thrust washer to wear, and eventually the possibly terminal grinding away of the rear face of the cylinder block. It would even be worth fitting a brake-pedal light switch to the clutch pedal to power a red light on the dashboard if you can't train yourself to keep your foot completely clear of the clutch pedal.

When replacing a clutch master cylinder, get an earlier pre-1970 item, of 0.75in diameter. Don't mix and match parts suppliers.

Clutch assemblies are either Laycock or Borg & Beck. The Laycock clutches are no longer available new although they can be found in reconditioned form. Borg & Beck clutches can either be exchange or new, new being preferable. Replacing OE clutch hydraulics can be a problem, as clearances and castings on the replacements can be rather random. It's possible to buy an adjustable slave cylinder pushrod from Girling, which has solved a good few squealing and slipping problems.

A good quality internal annular clutch-release system inside the bellhousing is an excellent idea, as the hydraulics as well as the bearing are protected from the elements. Annular release bearings get rid of the cross-shaft pin, and the old hose and slave cylinder, and they are more mechanically efficient, so they should give you a lighter clutch. If all goes well, this can work perfectly; however, if it doesn't go well, the gearbox has to come out again to get at the release system. On TR6 clutches, Randy Zoller likes to use a Toyota Land Cruiser release or throwout bearing, which is of good quality.

PROPSHAFTS AND REAR ENDS

When rebuilding and balancing, use the best quality universal joints available and pay the extra. Get them with grease nipples if possible, and if you are going to give your car any serious abuse, think about fitting a strap under and above the shaft at the front to stop it either dropping on to the road, or coming up and hitting your elbow if a U/J suddenly lets go.

Later Spitfire rear axles were as fitted to the GT6, and stronger. They offer the following potential rear-end ratios: 3.27, 3.89 and 3.63. Other than being rather small and

The update to a new rear-axle design with Rotoflex flexible rubber-drive doughnuts improved Triumph rear suspension, but finding quality replacement doughnuts can be a problem.

not absolutely adequate, the only recurrent mechanical fault aft of the gearbox is the Rotoflex couplings, rubber doughnuts that have to be regarded as a wearing part. Unfortunately, the quality of replacement parts is variable, and spares should be kept in reserve. If you get the option to buy expensive ones of better quality, do so and save money. Replacing the old shaft design with constant velocity joints is discussed in the suspension chapter.

The little Triumph differential has its limits. For standard Triumphs it gets by, but having a checked and overhauled spare ready in the garage would be a smart move.

Crunch, Crunch, Bang!

My own Vitesse once provided an intriguing mystery from the rear axle. Some rattling started, with no visible cause, then there was some intermittent clattering, still with no apparent cause, then some really nasty part-time clattering and finally a huge bang, followed by silence. None of this had any effect on the silky-smooth performance of the car. It turned out later that a propshaft bolt had come loose and fallen out, but every time I looked underneath, it happened to be at the top and out of sight. It's tempting to blame evil spirits.

For anything bigger than a 2500cc carburettored six, you'll have to get serious about the rear end. This is a Jaguar XJ6 rear axle on a custom frame under a 5-litre GT6.

Almost all suspension tuning starts with lowering the car, which lowers the centre of gravity, reduces body roll and usually involves stiffer springs, again reducing roll and improving stability.

5

suspension and steering

The first sentence of any chapter in any book on Triumph suspension will be about sorting out the suspect swing axles. There was, and is, a 'camber compensator' available for the rear suspension that is a quick and easy semi-cure for the wheel-lifting issues. It consists of a single leaf spring that attaches to the underside of the diff, opposite to the stock spring on top of the diff, and the ends go to anti-roll bar-type links on the outer suspension.

Lowering the ride height with blocks between the diff and the spring also helps, and changing the spring for a flatter and stiffer one resulting in more negative camber also helps. Buying a Mk IV Spitfire or a Mk II GT6 with factory improvements is another partial solution.

My Midge kit car weighs almost nothing at the back, and although the original transverse spring had half its leaves taken out, the back end was still wayward. With a Vitesse engine and an all-up weight of something like 1,300lb (590kg), the car was too fast for sub-Herald handling to be acceptable.

I changed the whole assembly for a Dolomite live axle.

The Midge had its own new chassis but it was still based on Triumph geometry: the new axle was mounted on trailing arms going between new upper and lower mounts on the axle casing and outriggers on the chassis. It was located sideways by a Panhard rod from the chassis to the axle, and it was fitted with coilover shocks, so the choice of shock hardness and spring rates was limitless. It has been a successful conversion, although it's fairly radical. If I were doing the same thing again, I would now think about using the back end of a Mazda MX5, which is independent, well engineered and strong, and comes in a very tidy and convenient subframe.

For anyone new to car tuning, the hardness of uprated shocks can provide a bit of a surprise. The different brands vary in their stiffness, but many are a lot more brutal than you might expect. If you're just looking to sharpen up your car a little, and replace old standard shocks with slightly more stiffness in the suspension, you might not like what you get at all. Even on minimum settings, some shocks are too hard. If the adjustment only goes between concrete

Olivier Martineau's car uses a ⁷/₈in Addco anti-roll bar at the back. They're called 'sway bars' in North America, which is a simpler name and avoids confusion between roll bars and roll-over bars.

hard and granite hard, that's not much of a choice. I'd definitely recommend joining a Triumph club in principle anyway, but one of the benefits is that you can ask to be taken for a drive in cars fitted with various shock absorbers and see what they feel like. No petrolhead will ever refuse to take somebody for a fast demonstration ride in their top toy.

If you like the sharp, flat handling provided by hard suspension, but don't like the battering your spine takes, you can achieve quite a good compromise by fitting better seats at the same time as stiffer suspension. Older Triumph seats have no head restraints and were basically designed in 1959, and things have moved on. If you don't fancy paying out on a set of heated and monogrammed Recaros, Mazda comes to the rescue. Mazda took full advantage of being handed the British sports-car market on a plate, and presented us with a really excellent British sports car – the MX5/Miata. Its admirable features include the seats, which are comfortable, supportive and small, and which fit our British-made British sports cars very nicely. Mazda's huge success over twenty-five years with their MX5 British clone means that thousands of scrapped examples now provide a good supply of cheap second-hand seats.

One thing to note is that you do get used to brutal suspension quite quickly. I used Marcos Heritage's demonstrator Mini Marcos for a long European trip, and it weighs about 1,000lb (450kg) and uses second-hand Mini mechanicals. The rubber suspension cones on later Minis harden into a concrete-like substance after a couple of decades. When they're fitted to a Mini Marcos, the 30 per

Olivier Martineau's car sets a good example. It has PRI adjustable shocks front and back: in front, 1in Addco sway bar; at the rear, ⁷/₈in Addco sway bar; and hard poly bushes throughout.

cent weight reduction automatically uprates the suspension ratings by a further 30 per cent, in addition to the age-hardened cones – so a standard Mini Marcos has virtually no suspension at all, apart from the tyre sidewalls. (Note that weight reduction stiffens suspension and improves handling on Triumphs as well, by the same physics.)

When I first drove the Marcos, I wondered if I'd made a big mistake in planning to drive a couple of thousand miles in a couple of weeks – but I soon got used to it, helped greatly by the good Marcos seats. The fun of the car's almost single-seater handling, and of not having to slow down for corners or roundabouts, outweighed the banging over bumps. Since then I've bought a Mini Marcos and am currently building it, although I will admit I've also bought a set of down-rated Smootharide suspension cones, and I'm using full-profile 145/80×10 tyres to get some depth in the sidewalls and some shock protection.

That may seem a tiny tyre with a tiny contact patch, but bear in mind that the car only weighs 1,000lb (450kg), and it needs small tyres to achieve any loading on the contact patch going into a corner. The rear corner weight on the right rear in a right-hand corner could be almost, or less than, zero, so spreading a very low weight over a bigger contact patch on a rough surface would not so much reduce grip as make it very variable. We don't like variable tyre grip and unpredictable contact patch loadings when going round corners quickly. Historical bodges include Hillman Imps with a layer of bricks loaded into their front boots, and factory Porsche 911s with lumps of cast iron bolted to the front to get some weight loaded on to the tyres.

Variable contact patch loading is precisely what you get when a Spit jacks up and puts the back of the car on one sidewall, so planning to avoid that happening is your first priority. All the above applies to a Spitfire, which has very little weight on the back tyres. Fitting wider tyres is literally the last thing I would do to a Spitfire's rolling gear.

ALIGNMENT AND ADJUSTMENT

The mysteries of suspension geometry are not rocket science. Camber is the angle of the wheels relative to the car – negative camber means that the bottom of the wheels are sticking out and the tops are leaning in. Spitfire rear wheels do that if the suspension has been lowered: they handle better because the tyre is pushed into a vertical position during hard cornering and the tread is flat and grips well. They also look better. Castor is another angle, but it refers to the front wheel hub: if an imaginary vertical line through the trunnion is grabbed at bonnet level and

An adjustable upper wishbone on this GT6 allows an instant change of camber to add negative and improve handling by bringing the wheel tops inboard. But too much negative will scrub the tyre edges.

leaned backwards, that's positive castor. Increasing positive castor makes the wheels self-centre and promotes stability, but increases steering weight.

Understeering on cornering is when the front end of the car hits whatever is in front of it, and oversteer is when the back end of the car hits what's in front of it. The design faults in our Triumphs cause both, for different reasons. If you're piling a Vitesse into a corner, there's too much weight on the front tyres because the engine is too far forwards. Applying more steering doesn't help: the front

The Herald's rear suspension has never been used by anybody else. QED

tyres lose grip, irrespective of which way they're facing, and you slither into the scenery front-first. The Vitesse has understeered. If you're piling an older Spitfire into a corner, the front will be fine, but the back suddenly jacks up, and rather than the back end being on two tyres, it's now only on one sidewall. There's no grip, the rear skids around in a spin and you head for the scenery backwards. The Spitfire has oversteered. Steering into the skid is technically taking steering off because the car is now oversteering: best of luck with that.

Bumpsteer is when the rack is not in the same plane as the wishbones and a road bump sends a shock through the steering wheel, but it only becomes a problem if the standard front geometry has been altered. The Ackerman angle you don't need to bother about, except that you shouldn't take any automotive advice from anybody who doesn't know what it is.

Alignment of the wheels is important. The tracking of the front wheels means that they should be rolling parallel or almost parallel to each other, otherwise they will scrub the tyres clean of tread in half an hour. Ideally you get all four wheels aligned at the same time: there are more adjustments available on a Triumph than on a modern car. A properly aligned car feels quite different and handles better, it uses less fuel and its tyres last longer.

ANTI-ROLL BARS

You really don't want to add harshness to the ride before you have to, so after the rear axle is tamed, the first improvement to make is a set of anti-roll bars or sway bars. When you go over a bump in a straight line, they

On a special that started as a Triumph-based GRP kit car and has now evolved into a spectacular aluminium-bodied special with a 2600cc Alfa Romeo straight six, the GT6 suspension is the only bit of Triumph still in place.

An anti-roll bar or sway bar usefully flattens out body roll without spoiling the ride, as it moves freely up and down unless cornering hard.

have no effect at all: they just hinge up and down. When you stuff the car into a corner, normally the wheel on the front outside of the corner goes up into one wheel arch and the other wheel comes down out of the other arch as the body rolls and tips over to one side, to the outside of the corner. The anti-roll bar resists this force, reducing the movement of the wheels as they relate to the chassis. Because the bar is sprung, it's not rigid but allows some movement, forming part of the car's suspension. The thicker the anti-roll bar, the stronger the spring effect, and the less rolling movement of the body is permitted.

SHOCK ABSORBERS

After the anti-roll bar come the shocks. I wouldn't recommend any that aren't adjustable, because performance shocks do tend to start off much harder than standard, and progressively winding them down to the softest setting is quite frequent. If buying from knowledgeable suppliers, try to get shocks that start off not much harder than standard. On the Mini Marcos I'm not even fitting uprated shocks, as standard Mini ones will already be uprated 30

Adjustable shock absorbers allow useful on-the-road tuning, but can be much harder than standard, even on soft settings. Posh ones have adjustable rebound settings as well.

This GT6 chassis, going under our featured Spit 6, has had the shock mounts extended to allow a longer action and more vertical positioning for the shock absorber, giving finer control and a better ride.
R. LAMBRECHT

The Rotoflex rear end is retained in a GT6-chassised Spit 6. There have been quality issues with replacement rubber couplings, so if you can find better and more expensive ones, go for those.
R. LAMBRECHT

per cent by the body's weight reduction. It is possible to buy shocks that are adjustable on the rebound as well as in compression: they're probably 'over the top' for a road car, though if you run heavy wheels – wires, for instance – you might benefit.

SPRINGS

Next in line for discussion are lowered springs. Lotus guru Colin Chapman preached soft springs and hard shocks, but the general trend is for lowered springs to be harder.

The suspension construction means it's easy to change front springs when you're experimenting to find the best compromise of ride and handling.

If you look at dedicated offroad buggies and bikes, their suspension movements are enormous and their springs soft. You can run into problems with shortened and therefore lowered springs of the original rating, because the car will tend to bottom out on bumps. Lowered springs have to be slightly harder, and commercial reality comes into it as well because those who buy lowered springs also want better handling and expect more suspension stiffness – so that's what they are sold. There is a substantial improvement in roll reduction to be achieved by lowering a car, and there's also a significant improvement in looks – almost any car looks better lowered. However, you will be banging the chassis and exhaust pipes off speed bumps, and will have to negotiate them crabwise.

It's not insanely expensive to have sets of springs made in particular lengths and strengths, to get precisely the response you're looking for: Springcoil in Sheffield makes custom car springs for £55 each, with a three-week lead time.

A probably apocryphal but usefully illustrative tale concerns an F1 driver, trying out a car with no springing at all, and the suspension locked up solid: 'It's very quick,' he is reputed to have said, 'but I can't keep my feet on the pedals.'

Lighter wheels are good, reducing unsprung weight, which makes the suspension work better. Of course a nice set of multi-spoke lightweight alloys doesn't do a Triumph any cosmetic harm, either.

POLY BUSHES

Hard polyurethane suspension bushes, fitted correctly so that they're not binding but are free to move, improve precision and actually allow the suspension to work as designed without the compromises of soft rubber bushes allowing play and slop and undesirable changes in geometry. They do, however, allow the transmission of harshness and jiggling from bad road surfaces, as they don't have the same cushioning effect as soft rubber bushes. Even good poly bushes are pretty cheap, though, so experimenting with them is affordable. If you find you don't like them, change back to new rubber bushes, which will still put you in a better place than where you started.

STEERING: RACKS AND WHEELS

The good front suspension and steering system on Herald-derived Triumphs mean you really don't need to make any changes. However, you can choose to fit a quickrack, which changes the rack ratio from 3.5:1 to 2.5:1, increasing the effect of turning the steering wheel by around a third. It also increases the weight of the steering by the same amount. In theory if you're racing, faster steering is good, but it also becomes heavy, twitchy, and possibly insensitive: steering movements tend to become jerky. You would get used to that, however, although if you're playing about near the edge of grip, clumsy steering movements might be counterproductive. Personally I've never felt the need for sharper steering on a Triumph: it's already very good.

Smaller steering wheels also add effort to the steering, and in combination with fatter radial tyres and a straight six, parking can become quite hard work. But many people like the feel of smaller and fatter steering wheel rims, and it's entirely a matter of personal choice. An expensive steering wheel does a lot for an interior, and Moto-Lita make some lovely wheels; they can also supply them unvarnished and unstained so that you can match them to your dashboard veneer colour. They once made me a custom thin-rimmed 15in woodrim wheel trimmed in black leather: that was expensive, but still not as expensive as a standard Nardi.

Quickracks – steering racks with a higher ratio and fewer turns lock to lock – are available, but it never occurred to me that any of my Triumphs needed one.

Spax adjustable shocks and new couplings under a GT6. As you can see, adjusting the shock settings just means a quick grovel under the car with a screwdriver.

Getting slightly jealous here: never mind the axle, look at the chassis – that's a fifty-five-year-old car and it still has no rust in it. The bone-dry SoCal climate has its benefits.

MOVING WEIGHT AROUND

Without getting too radical, improving the weight balance of a Triumph is worth thinking about. Moving weight from the front of the car to the back is good. The battery can go in the boot opposite the driver, the engine plates, brackets and so on can be light alloy, and if your bonnet is in rough shape, a GRP replacement bonnet could save 40lb (18kg) over a steel one, although if you go for the £300 rather than the £600 price zone, there will be some work required to make it look good.

Fitting different engines and moving the existing

A standard early Spitfire chassis with the suspension on display. Triumph's front suspension has been used by smaller mainstream manufacturers such as Reliant and TVR, and by dozens of kit-car makers. A high compliment.

New drive couplings replace the Rotoflex system. They're inherently a better design, and good quality components are available.

engine around in a car might not be regarded as either a suspension matter or an everyday modification, but I submit that they are very relevant, as engine weight and position are critical to handling. I was recently told that somebody local races a Vitesse, and my instinctive reaction was to say that would be a daft idea because the engine's in the wrong place. 'Oh, he moved it nine inches backwards,' was the reply. OK, that would make sense, I thought. This is after many years of driving assorted small Triumphs – Spitfires and GT6s with the later rear suspension are sports tourers, while the Vitesse is purely a tourer. It's hard work to drive one quickly, and it's telling that a GT6 with a small-block Ford V8 in it actually felt better balanced than a standard car. Having said that, the extra weight of the roof, glasshouse and tailgate on the standard GT6 means the weight balance and handling are not bad at all, after the rear axle has been sorted.

We can imagine the conversation between the engineering department and the accounting department at Triumph in 1961 about the Vitesse concept:

'Putting the big iron six with its iron head in a Herald would be nice, but we'd have to move the engine backwards.'

'Can't afford to do that. Too expensive.'

'Oh well, let's just bung it in anyway.'

When it comes to improving the suspension on a Spitfire or Herald, there are plenty of useful tweaks on offer, but I think you would get very good results for little financial cost in a 6-cylinder car by putting the engine in the right place. Apparently using Spitfire engine mounts on the Vitesse turrets moves the 6-cylinder engine backwards by

Spare axles are quite easy to source, and can be quietly overhauled and updated with new brakes and better couplings, then fitted at the next Rotoflex failure.

Moving body weight lower down in a car is a good way of lowering the centre of gravity and improving the handling. Changing to lightweight wood and GRP bodywork is a drastic but effective technique.

9in (23cm), which would make a major improvement to the balance of the car. Some considerable weekend effort would then be required to modify the propshaft, gearbox mounts, transmission tunnel, remote gear lever arrangements, plumbing and so on. The improvement would probably be more dramatic on a Vitesse, as the GT6 carries the extra weight of the roof, tailgate and glasshouse at the back, which was why it got the 6-cylinder engine in the first place, and the frontal engine weight actually balances it out quite well. The weight per front wheel on a GT6 is 550lb (250kg), compared to 480lb (220kg) on a Spitfire, so the difference is significant.

Olivier Martineau's Spitfire features multi-spoke alloy wheels and Wilwood calipers, on big drilled discs. With that level of cooling on a road car, he's not going to suffer from any fade problems.

brakes

Your first priority is to avoid disaster, so if your Triumph is early enough to have single-circuit drum brakes all round, you should certainly consider updating and upgrading to a later Triumph dual-circuit system. Fortunately, changing an early system for a later dual-circuit system merely involves a relatively straightforward brake-system rebuild and replacement, but you would definitely buy and/or overhaul a later dual-circuit master cylinder.

The principle of car braking is that non-compressible brake fluid transfers force from your foot along pipes and hoses to force brake linings or pads against a metal surface to create friction and stop the wheels revolving. In a single-circuit system, a leak from a corroded pipe means the brake pedal goes squishy as compressible air gets into the system, and after a small number of squishy brake-pedal movements, the pedal goes to the floor and you have no brakes at all. A complete and sudden failure of the brakes is rare, as it would have to be caused by a snapped hard line or an old hose bursting, but with a single system, the first sign of a squishy pedal is your only emergency warning.

In a dual system you don't lose all of the brakes, but depending on the design, you lose either one side, or the front, or the back. Losing the back brakes is relatively unimportant – in fact my 1978 Canadian-spec Mini has an OEM valve that disables the back brakes in an emergency – but losing either or both front brakes frequently means a crash.

Uprating a Herald or Spitfire to GT6 or Vitesse disc brakes is a good idea – the brakes as well as whole hub assembly are larger and stronger. You do have to change everything outboard of the wishbones, though, as there are size incompatibilities between parts. GT6 back brakes are also larger.

Uprating back brakes is mostly a waste of time. If they are in good condition and capable of providing 25 per cent of the power of the front brakes, and if the handbrake works all right, there is little point in achieving anything more. If you have massive front discs with multiple pots, it might be worth uprating the lining material on the back brakes. Aluminium rear drums with cooling fins are pretty

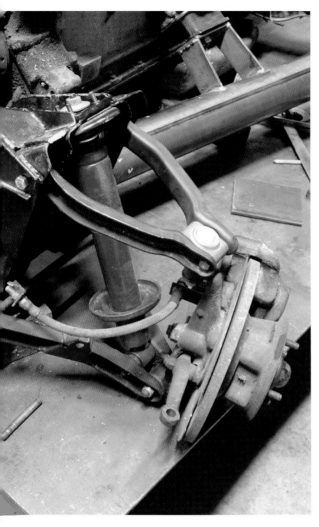

To upgrade a Spitfire, raiding a dead GT6 for its entire braking system represents good value. It's all a bit bigger and slightly more powerful. The whole front hub/upright/brake assembly has to be transferred to the old wishbones.

If you want to stick with drums but want sharper brakes, you can have your existing brake shoes relined with a softer compound of lining. This gets a more powerful braking action at the expense of a shorter life. From very soft forklift truck linings I'm expecting about 10,000 miles (16,000km).

and very expensive, but unless you're racing, they're just decorative.

If you have an original Herald or Spitfire and don't want to defile it with new-fangled disc brakes but could do with more retardation, here's a useful trick I've used on my 1938 MG TA, on which the brakes are pathetic: I had the shoes relined with forklift truck linings, which are very soft indeed. This has improved the brakes hugely, although I'm told the linings will only last for 10,000 miles (16,000km) or so. In the case of front drum brakes, finned ally drums would help – better cooling helps to reduce brake fade.

The next improvement would be in the brake pads. EBC Green Stuff seems to be very popular; this is specified for fast road use, but they have assorted other colours for heavier cars, for racing, and so on. They are made with Kevlar, and are reported as being grabby, long-lasting and low on brake dust.

More powerful racing pads can be a mistake, however. They may not work well until they're hot, which for a road car is all but useless. They may also chew up discs very quickly, as they often have a lot of metal in the pad material.

Servos I don't recommend, just from personal experience, although they might be appropriate for very high-performance multi-pot calipers, which could require more pedal pressure. Servos don't improve the brakes, they just reduce the pedal pressure required to operate them. The Vitesse that became my Midge came with a servo, and while servo assistance seemed merely pointless on the Vitesse – the standard brakes simply don't need a servo – it was actively dangerous on the Midge, on which the front brakes locked up the wheels with the slightest dab

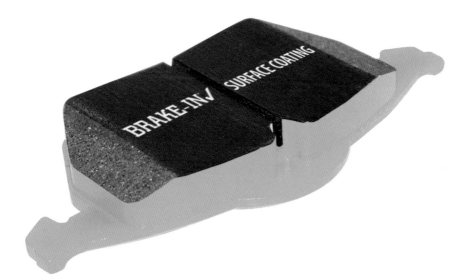

Green Stuff brake pads, as well as having a cool name, offer better braking grip but don't have to be warmed up like race pads. They have a good reputation.

on the pedal. I had transferred the whole Vitesse brake system into the Midge complete, but I removed the servo on the same day that I first drove the rebuilt car.

If you're fitting uprated calipers and discs, braked area is all important. Use the biggest discs you can get inside the wheels, and if they're vented, so much the better. Violently reducing the speed of a ton of car using friction generates a huge amount of heat, which will boil brake fluid and fade the brakes to uselessness unless it's effectively dispersed. Vented discs, which are essentially double discs with an air gap between them, are best.

There is controversy over drilling and slotting discs: they obviously lose a percentage of the grabbing surface, but some say they add cooling and disperse gases that come off red-hot pads. The original purpose of slotting was to scrape the glazing off the pads, but pad material design has improved since 1960. Research with a stop-watch during track days would not only establish the best solution for your car, it would be top fun as well.

When considering calipers, bear in mind that automotive fashion is very important to a lot of people, and the cool-looking and fashionable brands of caliper may not offer the best value. Wilwood calipers are apparently rather old-fashioned in appearance, but they traditionally offer a lot of braking per pound. At the time of writing, a Wilwood-based kit for the GT6 – including Wilwood Powerlite four-pot calipers, mounting plates, hardware and 265mm discs – was offered (new) on eBay for £400 including VAT.

Calipers that are long and narrow with lots of pots seem to work better than fat ones with fewer pots. Again, we're mostly looking for the maximum braked acreage at each wheel.

Stainless-steel brake hoses will give you a harder pedal, as the rubber hoses expand a little while transfer-ring hydraulic force. Be careful only to use stainless lines approved and sold for road use, though – the race ver-sions have a tendency for the steel wire to fray and wear

Discs or rotors eventually wear out, and can also warp if used enthusiastically; EBC, who make Green Stuff pads, also offer slotted and uprated discs at reasonable prices.

A set of Wilwood four-pot calipers, taken from a scrapped race car but currently resting. They would sharpen up the braking on a small Triumph very nicely.

through the inner nylon tubing, which then bursts and instantly disables either half or all of the braking system.

Silicone brake fluid sounds like a good idea, as it does not absorb water like ordinary brake fluid, and rusting cylinders are a very common cause of leaks and failure. Also, silicone does not destroy paint when dripped on it. However, there have been issues with old brake seals swelling and causing brake binding, and the quality and material specs of current cheap classic-market brake seals might be questionable with other than standard brake fluid.

AP Brakes won't go near silicone brake fluid, which gives one pause for thought.

SEALS OR NEW CYLINDERS?

Wheel cylinders are now very cheap, so fitting new seals may not make much sense. However, older components may be better made from better metals, so with new cylinders in place, you now have a couple of years to have the old cylinders bored out and repaired with bronze or stainless-steel inserts, which means that in practical terms they will last for ever.

The problem is that ordinary brake fluid is hygroscopic, and the resultant water descends to the bottom of the system – the wheel cylinders. It rusts them out, and the resultant rough surface rips up the rubber seals, which then leak. Seeping fluid also contaminates and writes off the brake linings.

Steel brake pipes also rust. Replacement involves making new ones with a brake flaring tool, but this is quite therapeutic, at least after you've got past the stage of flaring both ends of the pipe before remembering to put the unions on.

When bleeding the system, if you're trying to retain the existing iron calipers, apply a squirt of a mixture of transmission fluid and acetone to the bleed screw every day for a week before trying to undo them, or they will snap off. This is the best and cheapest releasing fluid in the world.

For credibility, period specials need large-diameter wheels. These are 15in MGC wires with tall, full profile radials, which worked well. Any size of wire wheels can be fitted to standard splined hubs, so skinny 2.5J ×19in MG wheels could be used. . . but 2.5in-wide wheels and 4.50 ×19 crossplies offer quite limited grip.

wheels and tyres

First, here is some critically important advice from techni- cal consultant Randy Zoller: 'Before going round any cor- ners at an angry speed, the puny ³/₈in wheel studs fitted to the smaller Triumphs *must* be replaced with larger TR3- TR6 wheel studs and nuts.'

If you're a concours obsessive and insist on the correct studs, replace old wheel studs with new, because your cur- rent ones have almost certainly already been damaged by a teenager in a tyre shop. Air hammer guns can apply random but massive amounts of torque up to several hundred lb ft, and stretched studs can and do randomly snap. You need to make tyre shops torque up your wheel nuts manually with a torque wrench. It's no good letting them whiz the nuts tight with the air hammer and check the torque with a torque wrench, because the torque wrench only indicates that the nuts are done up to, or beyond, the 43lb (19.5kg) it was set for, and the wrench will also click happily at 43lb even if the nut is done up to 150lb (68kg) or 250lb (113kg). If the shop won't use a torque wrench, either find a more professional shop, or

do it yourself. The recommended torque setting for small Triumph wheel studs and nuts is 38–48lb ft, and TR6 studs and nuts 80lb ft.

Second, it's good to be aware of offsets, which limit the options for wheel types and choices on our Triumphs. The offset means the position of the centre of the outer rim and the tyre relative to the hub. On rear-wheel-drive cars the offset tends to be negative, which means more of the rim is visible towards the outside, and the hub is inset. With modern front-wheel drive the offset is positive, so the rim looks fairly flat and the hub is out towards the edge of the car, with the wider bit of the wheels heading towards the centre of the car. The reason is that FWD involves the front wheels and tyres in trying to do several things at once, so various engineering bodges have to be applied to make FWD cars drivable. The rim offset bodge reduces the torque steer you get from putting power through the wrong wheels. FWD is cheap to make and improves cabin space, but proper sports cars are all rear-wheel drive.

Dramatic negative offsets look good and can offer

A very popular multi-spoke alloy in the USA is the Panasport. Its equivalent in the UK is Minilite, or copies thereof.

better grip with a wider track, but they do load up the bearings, driveshafts and hubs due to the extra leverage applied, so there can be a cost to that.

TYRES

Something to bear in mind is that the rear suspension of the Herald family was designed in 1958, and apart from contemporary exotic foreign Michelins, all tyres in 1958 for practical purposes were crossplies. Dunlop didn't even start developing radial tyres until the early 1960s.

Crossply or bias-ply tyres are substantially different in construction and characteristics from radial tyres. All tyres have cords in their structure, and in a radial-ply tyre, the cords are at right angles to the direction of travel, while crossply cords cross each other diagonally in the tyre.

The result is that the radial tyre has a stiffer tread and a more flexible sidewall, while the crossply has stiffer sidewalls and a more flexible tread area. The practical result is that the radial tyre is a major improvement on the crossply, with much more grip under all conditions. With a crossply, although there is much less grip, that loss of grip is progressive and more controllable. When you see vintage MGs being raced at Goodwood, they are drifting round every corner, using the controllable lack of grip as part of the technique.

Radials provide much better grip, up to a point, but then when they do let go, it's much more violent.

The original Zobo or Herald design called for 5.20×13

crossply tyres, fitted to 3.5J or 3½in-wide wheels. The contact patch is small and the grip levels quite low, but that's fine for casual general driving, and the steering is light and pleasant. The potentially evil rear suspension isn't usually a problem, as the tyres will probably gently let go before the axle jacks up. If you swerve in a 1960s Herald with radials, the grip is much better and the axle might well jack up, which means the rear end of the car lurches violently upwards and sideways.

Triumph's swinging rear axles are certainly a bad design, but we have to remember that they were designed to work with even worse tyres.

At the age of eighteen I did once swerve on the A3 going uphill past Putney Heath, in my grey fibreboard-dashed early Herald convertible, with three people in the car and the roof open, and it did jack up on me and very nearly turned over. As you can tell from the specificity of the location, it was a very memorable event. That would have been in 1972, and the car would definitely have been on radial tyres by then. Yes, that does make me officially an old man, but nearly everybody in life realizes in the end that it's worth listening to old men because some of them sometimes know whereof they speak. Of course, many don't.

So – avoiding jack-up is recommended, and if you drive an original Herald or Spitfire and don't want to alter and improve the suspension design, it might not be a bad idea to reduce the tyre performance to better match the suspension by backdating to a set of crossply tyres.

It also takes the car back to its original period feel and handling, which for many people is part of the fun. If you do change back to crossplies, the tracking at the front axle needs to be changed: with radials, toe-in is usually zero, but with crossplies the front wheels need to point inwards between $1/8$in and $1/16$in. I probably don't need to tell you that you have to change all five tyres, because it's dangerous and illegal to mix radials and crossplies on the same car.

If you go with radials, the 145×13 tyre size is slightly smaller than the standard 5.20×13 crossply size, and probably keeps more of the original feel and handling of the car, while the 155×13 size is slightly fatter.

Radials are not compulsory, though. You are unlikely to read that anywhere else, but let's think about it for a moment. With a car that we own for fun, the flavour and entertainment value of tyres can be more important than their performance. If we wanted efficient we'd buy a Kia/BMW/whatever. Here's an illustration. In a previous life I designed, and briefly manufactured, replicas of the gorgeous Jaguar XK120, using XJ6 mechanicals, my own chassis concept and a fibreglass body. My brother bought the prototype, which he ran on 15in wire wheels with Avon crossplies. He also owned a new turbo Subaru Impreza. He ended up always using the Jag for his daily country-road commute, because he was heading for losing his licence playing with the 140mph (225km/h) Impreza, but he could effortlessly and safely drift the Jag round corners in the wet without even breaking the speed limit. Yee–discreetly–ha. Modern drifting enthusiasts, who hunt

bad grip for fun, pump up their radials to 50–60lb to make them as hard and slidy as elderly crossplies.

If you decide to improve the suspension on your Triumph to match new-fangled modern grippy radial tyres, you will want to consider the implications of contact patch size. It's automatic for performance enthusiasts to fit wider tyres for more grip, and it usually works. However, very wide tyres on light cars run into a problem with the contact patch not being well enough weighted. Each tyre only contacts the road via a patch of rubber about the size of an iphone. Making the tyre bigger increases the size of the contact patch, but unavoidably decreases the weight per square inch that is concentrated on that patch.

The back end of a Spitfire isn't very heavy at all, and with modern performance tyres typically being 40 per cent wider than 1960s tyres, the physics dictates that you've unloaded each square inch of the contact patch by the same proportion. On a good smooth road surface you can charge around a fast corner nice and hard with the outside tyres beautifully loaded up, but a bump could unload them dramatically and unpredictably, in which case you'd better not still be driving on standard swing axles.

The other aspect of tyres, as it were, is the aspect ratio, which is the width of the tyre as it relates to the height. Old-school tyres are about 85 per cent as wide as they are high. As time went on and tyres became lower and wider, the extra aspect ratio number (the one in the middle) became more important – such as 165/65×13: this tyre has a 65 per cent aspect ratio, so it is 65 per cent as high as it is wide. A typical 2015 sports-car tyre size would be

Triumph Dolomite alloys use the common Spit family PCD, and at 5.5J×13 are quite fat compared to standard wheels. They would need spacers due to having the wrong offset, though.

225/45×18, which is dramatically different from an early Spit tyre of 145/85×13. Modern tyres are very wide, very shallow, and on a very big rim. Grip can be tremendous depending on the softness of the rubber compound, but the downside is that with low profiles and shallow side-walls, there is no suspension provided by the sidewalls as in taller tyres, and they are fragile and very vulnerable to bad road surfaces. Hitting a pothole could result in a £3,000 invoice as the shallow-sidewalled treads are crushed against the freshly bent rims. Seriously fashionable newer-car enthusiasts go even further, with tyres of 30 per cent profile.

Tyres of more than about seven years old should be scrapped, because rubber goes ever harder with age, and rock-hard old tyres, even with perfect treads, don't have very much grip at all. Keeping them in the dark helps, as the deterioration process is largely caused by ultraviolet light.

Triumph suspension is probably a little primitive for rubber-band ultra-low-profile tyres – Heralds don't have little computers electronically regulating the infinitely adjustable shock absorber rates on bump and rebound. In fact, 175/65×13 would probably be as big and wide as you would want to go. Tyre flexibility and flexion is part of the suspension equation, so although reducing tyre flexibility by reducing profile would initially take you back to crossply hardness, going to a too-low profile would bring in some harshness. Of course, stiff and low-profile tyres also offer a more direct contact with the road and more precision and grip, so if you really like sharp handling and don't care much about comfort, feel free to lower away.

Olivier Martineau pushed it to the edge with his wheels and tyres. Getting far away from 1959 and skinny 5.20×13 tyres, he fitted 15in Konig multi-spoke wheels with 195/50×15 Ventus tyres to his Spitfire. These will more or less fit the car at the back, but he says you have to roll the outer edge of the front wheel arches a little, and he also altered the camber for a bit more of a negative angle. Some negative camber is good for handling, but too much will trash the tyres fairly quickly, as it wears out the inner edges.

WHEELS

The standard steel wheels supplied with Triumphs got fatter as the years went by, as do owners and their cars – have you noticed that later models of VW Golfs and Ford Capris became progressively bigger and fatter at the same rate as their owners' waistlines? To some extent,

Olivier Martineau's Spitfire sits nose down on 15in Panasport alloys and low-profile Ventus stickies. Note the added rear anti-roll bar: this car will handle much better than a normal Spit.

bigger tyres offer more grip, so a very low-budget way of achieving wider wheels and tyres on older Triumphs is to nick them from newer Triumphs. Standard Spitfire wheel widths went from 3.5in to 4.5in and finally 5in.

However, the huge number of alloy wheels made in more recent decades has changed the whole picture. There were virtually no cars in 1959 with alloy wheels as standard, whereas now they're universal – you have to go seriously low-rent to avoid them on recent cars. The result is that you can buy Minilite lookalikes for £70 each, and

I'm refurbishing these period Revolutions, which is probably a bit daft because new ones are only £60 or so. You can't go wrong stylistically with black spokes and a polished rim.

Triumph's wheel stud PCD (pitch circle diameter) of 3.75in (95.25mm) is quite rare outside BMC/Leyland, but adapters can be used to take it to 100mm, offering a huge choice of wheels.

proper Minilites for £120. Panasport wheels are similar in style, and are popular in the USA. I'm currently refurbishing a set of period Revolution four-spoke alloys, which is actually fairly silly because I could buy new ones for £60 each from MiniSport.

It's always a good idea to keep unsprung weight as low as possible, because that way more of the weight of the car is under the control of the suspension, and the suspension itself is protected from the stress of a heavy wheel banging up and down, wearing out bearings and shocks. It also requires less effort to spin a lighter wheel, freeing more of the available engine power to make the car go faster. The open nature of alloy-wheel architecture also helps to get moving air in to cool the brakes. However, those of a cynical nature might want to literally weigh some of the wheel options before making a decision – a Spitfire 5J×13 steel wheel weighs 18lb (8kg) compared to my 5.5J×12 Revolutions at 10.5lb (4.8kg), but some of the more fashion-conscious alloy-wheel brands might value looking cool over being light and not save any weight at all. Of course you could just buy a set of wheels because they look nice. And why not?

Wire Wheels

Virtually all Triumphs look good with a set of wire wheels, except possibly the large saloons – though even those

Unusual hubcaps found on a Spitfire in the Pacific Northwest. They would get some attention at UK Triumph meets.

Wire wheels are actually of stronger construction than steel disc wheels or cast alloy wheels, although the central spline mounting baffles most tyre-shop balancing machines.

Bolt-on wire wheel hubs are attached in place of steel wheels, and are then progressively fully tightened and secured. The nasty-looking rust on that brake disc will be gone within a mile, no worries.

might look cool thus equipped. All the Triumphs discussed in this book certainly look fine on wires. From a styling point of view, chrome plating on wire wheels is generally regarded as a bit vulgar in the UK, although it's more acceptable in North America. However, bear in mind acid rain, salty roads, rusting chrome and hours of polishing.

The basic standard size of wire wheel for the Herald and Spitfire families is 4.5J×13 – a 4.5in-wide rim that is 13in high. Usually a 155×13 radial tyre or a 5.20×13 crossply would look right. The hubs and the single-splined fittings on the wheels are available in just a few sizes related to the size of the car they're on, so once the 42mm Triumph-spec hubs are on, you can fit a variety of larger and fatter tyres and 42mm-hub wheels, as long as you can get them under the wheel arches without fouling.

Some small Triumphs would have been fitted with wire wheels as an option from new, but Motor Wheel Service (www.mwsint.com) offers two ways of achieving wire wheels on wire-less cars. Bolt-on wire wheels are simpler and cheaper than getting involved with splined hubs. The bolt-on style wire wheels are not laced to a spline, but to a central plate like the middle of a steel wheel, which has four holes in it at the right PCD or 'pitch circle diameter' (the diameter of the wheel stud pattern) for the standard Triumph disc-wheel hubs. These simply bolt on in place of a steel wheel. In a silver-painted finish they cost about £150, similar to a splined wheel, plus tubes, tyres and VAT. In chrome they cost another hundred pounds or so. They have to be bolted up to a high 75lb of torque.

For more 'proper' splined knock-off wheels, the system is different. If you have a car with original splined wire-wheel hubs and they are still in good condition, you just check the hub condition, smear on a little copper grease, pop the new wheels on and tighten up the spinners: job done.

If your car has standard steel wheel hubs with four conventional wheel studs, you can fit bolt-on splined hubs that are designed to provide a hub suitable for wires, and then you slide on a set of 'proper' wire wheels. The splined hubs are bolted on first in place of wheels, and then the original studs usually have to be shortened. The new hub nuts will probably have to be tightened up a few times – you'll hear and feel when they begin to come loose – and they will then be centre-punched between the bolt and the stud thread to secure them permanently. The wire wheels then just slide on to the splines and are secured by chrome spinners, which are hammered on with a soft mallet, and much more gently than you would expect: they don't need much torque to hold them on firmly. The spinners are cut in right-hand and left-hand threads to suit the direction of travel, which takes getting used to. You can opt for spinners without ears, which are tightened up with a large spanner and are less likely to be stolen or deliberately loosened by anyone jealous.

At the time of writing, hubs from MWS are £35 each plus VAT, and the chromed brass spinners each cost £18 plus VAT. Chromed knock-off wire wheels for centre-splined hubs cost £158 plus VAT, compared to £107 for silver-painted wires. With bolt-on wheels that attach to

The proper wire wheels slip on and are held on by single central spinners. This was a Triumph special but it's now evolving with many Alfa Romeo bits – there's not much Triumph left in it.

steel wheel, four-stud hubs, the chromed variety cost £242 each plus VAT, while painted ones are £165. Shiny bling has become more expensive of late: wire wheels used to be very well priced when they came from Dunlop in India, but that goes back a while. To convert a Spitfire or other small Triumph to a new set of knock-off wires and tyres would raise an invoice heading for about £2,000.

Buying wire wheels secondhand has to be done carefully, because splined wire wheels do wear out – the splines inside the hubs take a beating from braking and acceleration. Unlike steel disc wheel studs with the nuts torqued up tight, the wire wheels have to start off with a little free play between the splines on the wheels and those on the hubs, or you would never be able to get them on or off. After a couple of decades of accelerating and braking, they get sloppy. The hubs wear out first, but the wheels eventually wear out too. My pre-war MG originally had about 30 degrees of slop on one hub. With wheels jacked up and braked, check any secondhand wheels for slop on a hub that has good splines, before buying them. Refurbishment of worn wire wheels is possible, but new wheels are usually a cheaper option.

Bear in mind that any old secondhand Triumph with wire wheels automatically has secondhand hubs and splines – so with the brakes on and each wheel jacked up, check for slop.

To check wire wheels for condition, you need to check the 'wobble'. This is measured on the rim inboard of the edge by taping something like a sharp screwdriver or pencil to an axle stand, placing it by the wheel and posi-

tioning the sharp end to just touch the wheel rim. Then rotate the wheel until there is a gap between the tip and the rim, and measure the gap with feeler gauges at its widest: if it's less than 0.094in you're in business; otherwise the rim is outside Triumph's tolerances.

Balancing wire wheels can be tricky. When mounting them on a balancing machine, there are specific bearing surfaces at the back of the wheel and where the nut locates, and attempting to balance a wire wheel using universal steel-wheel balancing cones is worse than useless. If your chosen shop doesn't have special wire-wheel mounting cones they can't do the job. The good news is that old-fashioned static balancing with an air bubble is very likely to do the job to your complete satisfaction. The best possible option is to get the whole rotating assembly dynamically balanced, but it's now unusual to find anyone who can do that.

Some people think that wire wheels are weak, but that's an old wives' tale. Smacked on a kerb, they'll do a lot better than alloys, and after the rim edge has been straightened with a hammer, they can often be trued up by tightening the spokes, just like a pushbike wheel. The front wire wheel on my Vitesse special hit a Sierra on a roundabout, and although the spinner made a bit of a mess of the Sierra, the wheel was undamaged. The only real damage to the Midge was to one trackrod, which was bent at a right angle. The steering rack still worked fine, but I thought it wise to get a new one. The wire wheel – and the spinner – were completely undamaged other than having collected some paint from the Sierra.

The basic chassis design common to Heralds, Vitesses, GT6s and Spitfires. This one is from an abandoned GT6 project, and is in the process of losing its outriggers in preparation for a new body and a life as an Alfa Romeo special.

8

structure and interior

THE CHASSIS

A Triumph of our type has to be in a much worse state of deterioration than most cars before it is truly scrap, because it has a proper chassis. The chassis does rust, but both the bodywork and the chassis have to be seriously bad before you would give up.

MOT regulations are tightening up, and you are now not allowed any rust near to any suspension components or attachments. However, this is best regarded as a positive and welcome raising of the bar rather than a nuisance, because higher standards of annual repair demands will keep our classics alive for longer. My 1978 Mini is quite possibly scrap because I haven't had to repair it for annual MOTs, and after eight years of further rusting it may now have deteriorated too far.

Mind you, there's actually no good public safety rationale for annual car testing. Canadian research found no statistically significant accidents caused by car condition – crashes are caused by carelessness, drinking and

immaturity, and rust doesn't come into it. However, civil servants in the UK and Europe have to find something to do, and continuous fiddling with car regulations keeps them looking busy. MOT standards are also very variable, and you might well find that a different MOT station will yield quite a different result.

So let's be positive about it. Banging with a (small) hammer all over a chassis before the annual MOT will reveal anything unpleasant that needs sorting out, and in most cases a competent welder will be able to repair the chassis by cutting out the rust and inserting new metal.

With Heralds and Vitesses, a strong chassis is really all that's needed – the bodywork is not structural. MOT requirements may require Heralds to have bodywork with no holes in it, but structural safety doesn't. Having said that, small Triumphs are not good cars in which to have big accidents.

In contrast to Herald/Vitesses, the sills on Spitfires and GT6s definitely do need to be solid. There are no outriggers on the sports-car bodies, and the sills need to be solid

The chassis under our Triumphs is simple and substantial, and even fairly significant rust can usually be successfully repaired.

An early Spitfire tub is restored by British Heritage Motorsports in San Diego for concours competition. With no outer chassis legs, Spitfire sills need to be solid, whether for shows or shopping.

This is how it should be done, but the Spitfire is a simpler structure than, for instance, an MGB, and a successful home restoration is a very achievable project.

both to pass MOTs and to be reasonably safe. There are twelve mounting points that attach the Spitfire body to the chassis, and they all need to be sound. This is a point that will come up again, but with the low cash values of Spitfires in particular, it will always be cheaper to buy a completely solid Spitfire than to have a rusty one repaired. Unless you do it yourself, restoration will usually be much more expensive than buying another and better car.

One point to make is that there are many abandoned projects about, so it's very possible to find a better tub secondhand, saving all the aggravation of welding a rusty one back together again. Having sorted out the rust, it's worth taking advantage of modern chemical treatments such as POR-15 to delay the next onslaught of rust for as long as possible.

Spitfire Dick has broken up dozens of Spitfires to build a few really nice ones. His back garden is full of usable chassis and body tubs. These remain fairly easily available.

RUST AND WELDING

Gas welding and TIG welding are quite difficult. With TIG in particular, the machines are expensive, and you have to manipulate a length of thin welding rod, a handle with a button and a foot pedal, all delicately and all at the same

Welding machines are now cheap enough to be very affordable: this sort of thing would cost a couple of hundred pounds, although spending £300–£400 would get you a better machine and probably better value.

time. Multi-tasking and delicacy are not the natural remit of blokes, and women, although better equipped for both, are not usually first in the queue to spend their weekends sitting on a cold garage floor welding bits of ancient cars back together again.

There are three pieces of good news, though. The first is that in contrast to the other techniques, MIG welding is genuinely quite easy to do adequately. The second is that the machines are cheap – a few hundred pounds buys a

Pressing the trigger operates an electric motor that feeds wire along a tube and into the weld, where electrical power melts it into whatever you're welding.

An inert gas, in this case argon blended with CO_2, flows down the tube and excludes oxygen, ensuring a clean weld. MIG welding is fairly intuitive and the basics are easily learned: achieving solid welds on Triumph bodywork is definitely achievable.

sensible mid-range amateur MIG welder. Cheap MIGs are fine for experienced welders, but beginners should buy mid-priced kit to be sure that inadequate equipment is not causing extra difficulties.

The third piece of good news is the availability of the instant-darkening welding helmet, which means you just

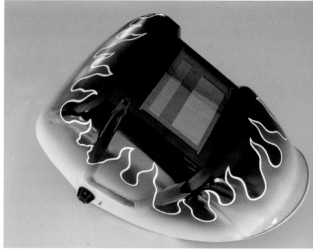

Modern welding helmets have instantly darkening lenses, so you can just look at the work and then spark up the machine – so much easier than flipping hinged glass or the whole helmet up and down every ten seconds.

This is the most appallingly bad piece of welding I've ever seen, perpetrated by a 'professional' exhaust shop. However, although it looks atrocious, it still did the job, which is encouraging for the more inept.

Welding is actually mostly grinding, particularly in the early stages, in the same way that tennis beginners spend most of their time walking around picking up balls.

position the welding tip and go for it – no more flipping masks down, which always moves the tip out of place. Not using a proper welding mask is insane, as the intense light flash from welding burns permanent blind patches in your retinae.

Welders and grinders should be regarded as one tool, really, and there is much more grinding than welding at the beginning, as your mistakes all have to be ground off. Letting patches of new metal into visible outer panels is a bit advanced, and you would have to take some time to learn to MIG-weld well enough to do that, but although adult education in the UK has taken a serious downturn, there is still the occasional evening welding course to be found, or there will be somebody in your local club or pub with welding experience, or competence can be achieved via Youtube, or even through trial and error. There is no reason at all why you couldn't weld new panels on to a body, or make safe and solid repairs to floors and chassis outriggers, within quite a short time. If I can do it, so can you.

THE TRANSATLANTIC RUST SIDESTEP

One rather good idea for achieving rust-free bodywork is to buy the best Spitfire or GT6 you can find in California or Nevada, inland Oregon and Washington, or Arizona and New Mexico, where there are still Triumphs that are completely free of rust. Prices in the USA, even for a good Spit, are low, and you might also find a GT6 at a good price. There are few Heralds and Vitesses, however, as they weren't imported to North America in great numbers.

Most British sports cars, including Spitfires, were built to be exported to North America, and many of them are still there. If they're in a dry state, many of them remain pretty well corrosion free – the downside is that the same sun that protects the steelwork also destroys the plastic interior and wooden dashboards. However, compared to a total body restoration and replacing sections of rotten chassis, it is relatively easy to change a crumbled and baked desert interior for a completely new one, either from classic Triumph interior suppliers or from a rusty UK scrap Spit with a nice interior and dashboard from under greyer and gentler skies. A complete interior transfer would take a weekend, even including new seat covers, while a proper amateur body and chassis restoration usually takes a couple of years.

Conversion to right-hand drive of an earlier Spitfire with the central instrument panel is relatively easy, as they were designed to be easily built in either format anyway. Having said that, driving an LHD car in your own country isn't too big a problem – you get used to it quickly, and the issues are minor. For example, for A-road overtaking either you need to lean over the two feet required to put your

A Spit 6 approaches completion. After a nice professional paint job it's being reassembled with considerable care. Whites and creams are good colours for home resprays because they cover up a multitude of sins.

Lots of replacement period goodies such as bullet mirrors are still available. Holden Vintage and Classic carry many such Christmas presents as well as practical lighting and electrical bits and pieces.

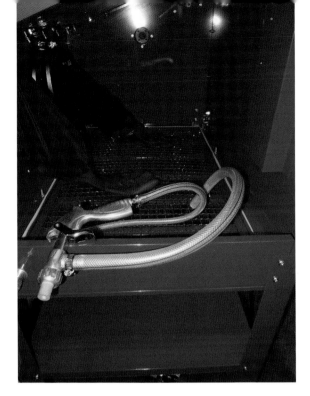

A blast cabinet and compressor are very useful pieces of kit, if you have any notion to restore a Triumph. Making small metal components look brand new again takes seconds.

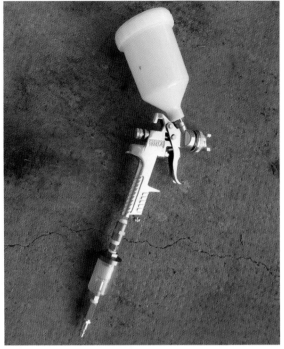

Once you have a compressor, logically you're ready to spray-paint either bits and pieces or your entire car. Buy a better spray gun than I did, for around £150; I bought this cheap one and it's a bit spattery.

head in the right place for seeing past slower cars prior to overtaking, or you can back off, which is better technique anyway, and pull over a bit further. Going into automatic-ticket car parks is a nuisance, but you can either stretch up from a Spit, or you can drive in and out backwards, which is rather fun anyway.

The buying-in-America idea doesn't make so much sense if you just fly out, buy a car and have it shipped back, but if you buy one, use it for a touring holiday for a few weeks and then ship it back, which would represent a great deal of fun per pound. Avoid high summer in California, though, as the heat can be brutal. Hagerty

A hardtop is a good way of reducing noise, weather and water ingress to make a Spitfire a year-round car. Steel factory roofs are expensive and heavy. Don't buy one in October/ November, as prices double and availability vanishes.

Smiths can still overhaul their own instruments, and they have some attractive alternatives as well: check out the Cobra range (www.speedycables.com).

Insurance tell me that they will offer insurance and breakdown cover for such a trip.

ADDING LIGHTNESS AND FIBREGLASS PANELS

Colin Chapman did quite well with his policy of adding lightness to Lotuses, and you can apply the same techniques to either rusty Triumphs or those that you want to make faster. In principle, for more performance you need to get rid of weight outside the wheelbase and high up, and the first place to start is reducing unsprung weight – so genuinely lighter alloy wheels are the first step. Moving a 6-cylinder engine back towards the centre of the car is ideal, but quite a big project. Moving the battery to the boot is worthwhile. It wouldn't be worth changing if you already have one, but looking for a fibreglass hardtop rather than the factory steel one would save weight and money, although the factory hardtops are much nicer than aftermarket GRP ones.

The weight saving from changing a presumably rusty steel Spitfire front end for a fibreglass replacement is about 16kg (35lb), and you can also opt for the GT6 front end (£295) with the power bulge, which is simply prettier. You can also replace the doors with fibreglass (£95, inner and outer panels), bootlid, valances and other panels, with a similar weight saving pro rata. Those bits will also not rust again, although the rest of the car obviously still will (www.honeybournemouldings.co.uk sell a lot of GRP Triumph panels).

Just fitting one or two GRP panels reduces value, as it looks cheap. If you go the whole way and change everything you can, that will definitely make the car go faster, and it can be presented as structured and deliberate performance improvements – in this case it's not bodged, but lightened for better performance.

The status politics of fibreglass replacement panels on classic cars is complex. Whether or not it's acceptable depends partly on the price and status of the car. GRP is a better material out of which to make cars if you want them to last, but it can do dramatic damage to values on more expensive cars. The front wings on my steel MK IV Bentley have been fatally fibreglassed from underneath, which has meant creeping damp and probably terminal rust. Steel replacements are £5,000 each – for a car that's worth £15,000 in running condition. GRP replacements would be sensible, but nobody who wants a Bentley wants a Bentley with plastic wings: it's just not something one does with Bentleys.

If you want to enter your Triumph in any sort of car show, and if you want it to be capable of winning prizes when you've finished it, you can't have any visibly fibreglass panels on it. Purists get very snotty about plastic. However, for a car that's in general use, and that has a decent chassis beneath it, fibreglass panels are very sensible. Replacing rusty front valance panels with plastic ones on all Spitfires is a fine idea – they take a beating from salt and grit, and once the better quality GRP panels are painted, it would be very difficult to tell what they're made of, apart from the absence of rust bubbles a few years later.

Plastic flip fronts on all the Triumphs we're concerned with are much cheaper than any professional repairs of steel panels, but you get very much what you pay for, and many of them don't fit very well. Glassfibre Triumph fronts are all a slightly different shape anyway – they're not rigid to start with, and they were all moulded from original steel bonnets of varying shapes. The fit of a new front end to your particular scuttle and doors may end up with yawning Range Rover gaps that will whistle like a Volvo.

With cutting and re-gelling, you can make GRP panels fit beautifully, and it is easy if unpleasant work, but if you're really concerned about panel fit you might be better to buy a £250 MIG welder and repair a steel front instead.

REPLICA LE MANS SPITFIRE BODYWORK

A recent development could be of interest to those who find themselves with a terminal, previously skilfully

The MkI GT6 bonnet features cooling louvres that were deleted in the Karmann update and revision. A shame, as they added both cool and cooling.

T6 Le Mans body is fitted to a Triumph chassis, replicating the successful 1960s Triumph Spitfire 24 endurance racers. It shares many lines with the GT6 body, but is in lightweight GRP with no tailgate.

12/50 Heralds came with a Webasto full-length sunroof, which in many ways is much better than a convertible top. This rare NOS Webasto was found in New York for $500, but Brits can still hunt down scrap 12/50s and take their roofs, and Webasto still offer overhauls from £350.

bodged Spitfire or GT6 body. There are dishonest people about who have the skill to craft what looks like excellent bodywork out of chickenwire, newspaper and filler. Ironically, this takes about the same amount of time and skill as doing the job properly, but it can ensure the car's doom as the rust creeps behind the filler, which remains permanently damp and invisibly corrodes the steelwork until the car is wet toast.

A good number of Triumph owners will still start repairing what looks like a few rust bubbles or a little crack, and will end up levering out huge chunks of filler on to a driveway red with terminal rust. Quite often, however, the chassis will still be either solid or easily repairable, and a good option at that point is to look for a solid, or at any rate repairable, secondhand bodyshell. Fortunately, eBay is still relatively rich with abandoned Triumph restorations, and often the body welding has been completed.

You can also now build a body-rusted scrap Spit with a solid chassis into something that's still a Spitfire but decidedly more interesting – a replica of the Le Mans Spitfires of

The bonnet of the T6 Le Mans isn't shared with the GT6, but has its own look and very effective aerodynamics. Fuel economy of 22.4mpg (12.6ltr/100km) at 94.7mph (152.4km/h) round Le Mans can't be bad.

the 1960s. These Triumphs were a great success. They were lightweight coupé bodies, weighing between 1,600lb (726kg) and 1,700lb (771kg) all in, with 1100cc engines producing 100bhp. In the 1964 Le Mans event, three cars were entered: two crashed, but the third one came third in class with an average speed of 94.7mph (152.4km/h) and fuel economy of 22.4mpg (12.6ltr/100km). There were even better results in 1965, with four cars entered: one crashed, one broke, but the remaining two came first and second in class, with the faster one coming thirteenth overall against Ferraris and Porsches. Top speed, which would have been recorded along the Mulsanne straight before the introduction of the spoilsport chicane, was 140mph (225km/h), with an average speed of 95.1mph (153km/h).

This rather magnificent effort deserved recognition, which has now come in the form of the T6 Le Mans replica body kits, which are essentially a GRP body conversion and bonnet for a Spitfire. The resulting car looks quite like a GT6, but is a good replica of the Le Mans Triumphs. It has pleasing detailing, such as 3D cutouts on the dashboard for the instruments. The price for the shell, doors, bonnet and all requisite body panels is under £7,000, and with the right donor, that would buy you quite a lot more than just a replacement and permanently rust-free Spitfire body – with a decent engine, you would be looking at similar performance numbers to the 1960s race cars. Nowadays we have the advantage of converting to, or staying with, the later rear suspension, after which you would have a fast road car and a very capable track-day toy.

The body is held in place with eight bolts, so although the complete replacement of the body might be regarded as more than an everyday modification, it's far from rocket science. By the time a complete novice has stripped, cleaned, inspected, sorted and painted the donor Spitfire chassis and mechanicals, tackling the rebuild of the body as a Le Mans replica would be easy (www.Triumphspitfirelemans.com).

KIT-CAR BODYWORK

The Le Mans body above is somewhere between a kit and a replica, but there are still, even now, some current Triumph-based kit-car options. This book is about Triumphs rather than kits, but I'd suggest having a look at some of the options before dismissing the idea. Kit cars offer strong, corrosion-resistant and lightweight body options, but retain plenty of Triumph DNA and are welcomed by clubs and usually surrounded by admiring crowds. To be frank and slightly subversive, there's a limit to how long one can spend admiring a gleaming line of identical standard Triumphs, and it's the offbeat that gets the attention.

Currently, after an unusually incompetent introductory government shambles, there is a very expensive, pedantic and rather silly UK government test applied to new kit cars, but it doesn't apply to cars that retain their original chassis. Hooray for Triumph! Kit cars that are already registered are also unaffected, and over the years many Triumph-based kit cars have been properly registered.

You can do what you like with fibreglass. This Corsa Spyder kit is having its entire cockpit shifted backwards by 9in (23cm) or so to improve its visual proportions, supervised by Miles Fenton (see Chapter 1).

'. . .a gleaming line of identical Triumphs.'

Many of the kit body options have 1930s-inspired designs, such as the Midge of which you've seen photos in this book. That's a low-budget, plywood-construction, plan-built design, still available from the Midge Owners' and Builders' Club, which now has the rights to the design (www.mobc.co.uk).

The Gentry is a replica of the pre-/postwar MG TD or TF, with a mix of fibreglass and wooden panels, and has been on sale off and on for so long that it's almost a classic itself (www.gentrycars.co.uk).

Moving forwards in time to the 1950s and 1960s, the Sammio is a more enclosed design reminiscent of the fibreglass bodies supplied for fitting to Austin and Ford rolling chassis, which had designs that vaguely referred to contemporary 1950s sports racers such as Maseratis and Aston Martins (www.sammio.co.uk).

As these vehicles no longer look like a Triumph, but still use the chassis, axles, engine, transmission, steering assembly and suspension from the donor Triumph, they become a classic re-body rather than a new car. They require a V627/1 form to be filled in, and a brief engineer's inspection. If you buy an old Triumph-based kit secondhand and in need of some attention, there are some astonishing bargains about, and any Vitesse-based kit originally intended for a 1200cc engine, but fitted with a 2000cc engine, will go like a hungry cheetah. Insurance premiums are also usefully low for kit cars, as people who build their own cars tend not to crash them.

Another fine and comically underpriced kit car is the Gentry, with abandoned projects coming up for a few hundred pounds and good roadworthy examples for a few thousand. It's an MG TF lookalike, but with optional Vitesse power.

The Sammio Spyder is one of a range of fibreglass bodies to fit Triumph chassis. They're designed in the style of 1950s specials and refer to the Italian sports cars of the period.

Nowadays it's a smart move to lock Spitfire and GT6 bonnets shut, when there are expensive and shiny things inside. You can also lock the bonnet shut on a battery cut-off switch, introducing complications and delay, neither of which thieves like.

ROLL-OVER BARS

Single-hoop roll-over bars are all right if you're planning just to roll over while stationary. If you might still be moving forwards quickly at the time, an unbraced roll-over bar is going to be of limited effectiveness unless it's massive as the forces trying to fold it flat in a crash are quite substantial. Any roll-over bar is better than none, but to be seriously strong, it needs to have brace bars going backwards or forwards, from quite high up: the strength

Always good to see a rollover bar, although for some reason rollover crashes are much more a North American thing: the British have roundabouts and 50 per cent fewer road deaths than Canadians.

On examining the car more carefully, the rollover bar isn't really well braced backwards, so it would be of limited use in a big accident, when it might fold flat.

The Spit 6 has a more substantial rollover bar, but it's still not braced until below the level of the bodywork.

The structure below the bodywork is very solid indeed, but while it's probably stiffening up the bodywork nicely, it still needs the top triangulated.

This GT6 has a hefty rollover bar, which is actually properly braced backwards – combined with having a solid roof as well, anybody in the car will merely be inconvenienced by a rollover.

is in the triangulation. We're only talking about sports cars here, rather than racing cars, but some of us can get going a bit sometimes. As I've been aware of the limitations of single bars for some time, I've noticed that my track-day driving becomes much more dashing with a proper braced set of roll-over bars.

INTERIORS

The replacement of interiors in Triumphs is usually fairly simple, whether you're changing for a less unattractive secondhand interior or upgrading to a new one.

My first recommendation would be to think about

The Spit 6 has kept the best bits of the GT6, including the seats, now trimmed in black leather. These are only going to look better as the years go by.

Olivier Martineau's original seats have been retrimmed. There is no reason why you should stick to correct Triumph patterns – they're not cars with high cash values, which frees us to enjoy them any way we want.

Earlier Spitfires were fairly basic inside, and the weight was deliberately kept down. Bigger engines and interior woodwork came along later.

Kit-car suppliers such as Europa are used to providing small and well designed seats for small spaces such as Triumph cockpits, although Spitfire and GT6 seats really are very small, so you're restricted to a very limited number of seats that will fit: arm yourself with measurements to find out what options are on offer.

The original Triumph seats were quite well made compared to Minis or other contemporary cars, and rebuilding them to look good is apparently rather trickier than some. By the time you've replaced the foam, the webbing and the seat skin itself, the bill from Newton Commercial will be impressive. Newton is the king of interiors, with good quality materials that are inevitably not cheap. Their experts, with decades of seat building, can re-skin a seat in an hour, whereas most of us will spend at least an afternoon getting it to look like a seat; nevertheless, with patience it can be done. There are also cheaper materials options on the market.

Your first attempt at stuffing a seat skin may well end up looking like a pillowcase full of badgers. None of it is unachievable, though. The seat is a simple tubular steel frame with elastic webbing stretched across it, followed by glued-on foam padding, and then a sock stretched over the foam and clipped and glued in place. Getting the skin stretched evenly over the foam is the tricky bit, but you just have to persist with pushing the foam into place and pulling the skin over the padded frame until it ends up looking like a seat.

Rebuilding the existing seats is well worthwhile, and if you're looking for an upgrade there are leather covers available. One point to make about leather is that the colours age differently – magnolia leather looks exotic and flash when new, but before long it starts looking sad. Black and dark colours, conversely, only look better and better as they acquire patina and wisdom.

Rebuilding seats with new covers is reasonably achievable, although getting the covers to sit well on the foams requires much patience and calm music – Pat Metheny is good for this, and early Floyd. Initially the seats will look grotesque, but the covers can eventually be stretched and pulled and twisted into looking like seats again. The foams and straps and covers and glue can all be bought from Newton, which although expensive, is very good kit.

If your budget doesn't stretch to new leather, it could be very useful to know that both new and old vinyl can be cheaply and very successfully re-coloured: in which case you can cheaply and easily assemble a good interior, located at autojumbles and from fellow club members, of completely random colours, and therefore bought for next to nothing: a single mismatched door panel is almost

replacing the original seats: they're not bad compared to some, but there has been progress in seat design since 1958, and an excellent option on a budget is to steal a set from a Mazda Miata. These are small, neat, cheap and very comfortable indeed, although they're more padded than the standard seats so you sit a little higher.

There's also the matter of a broken neck in a rear-end crash – as far as injuries go, it doesn't get worse than that. It will always be worth upgrading to a high-backed seat with a head-restraint function, even if you just change to another later Triumph seat.

Budget sports/competition seats are also a good idea.

worthless. When you have a set of good seats and trim, aiming for seats with head restraints for safety reasons if your originals are the old low-back type, you can re-dye the whole lot in the colour of your choice. Literally – you can go black, white, whatever you want. I recently dyed a couple of white seats black just to make the point.

Aftermarket retractable seatbelts are the smart move. The originals, if your Triumph is fitted with any, would work after a fashion, but although they're better than nothing, they won't be pulled tight enough to be effective. They are a wearing part and should be replaced as soon as they look less than perfect. You wouldn't risk

A dramatic demonstration of re-dyeing vinyl seats. These were both white before one of them was attacked with cleaner and a can of spray vinyl dye. They're ex-Suzuki Jeep, and might work well in a Triumph.

More swatches of home-dyed vinyl – it was dyed in the first place, and it takes very happily to any new colour you care to use: it sinks in below the surface properly and doesn't flake off like paint.

The GT6 is also equipped with a racing fuel cell rather than just a fuel tank, so the owner can feel free to have a big crash without any worries at all.

driving on forty-five-year-old tyres, and the same applies to belts. Securon makes easy-fit retractable sets for all our Triumphs. This being 2016 and the USA being overrun with lawyers, I wouldn't make any recommendations as to providing an upper seatbelt mount in cars that don't have one. In my last MGB I fitted a roll-over bar and welded a shoulder mount on to that at a comfortable level, and on my 1958 Chevy Delray I have personally chosen to weld upper seat-belt mounting plates to the B pillars. The pillars are not very strong, but if I hit anything hard enough to bend them, I'd rather be wearing a belt than not.

NEW-FANGLED MODERN SCIENCE

Computers have not improved life, they have merely made it faster and nastier. However, some progress since the 1970s has been forwards rather than backwards or sideways, and that includes chemical rust prevention and sound-deadening materials. Substances such as POR15 are a great improvement over the original Triumph rust-prevention techniques, which were either nothing, or a coat of hard underseal that cracked and allowed in damp, and thus encouraged truly rampant rusting. Once your car is properly rust repaired, and with ongoing paint chips touched up quickly, the new anti-rust materials will protect it much better. Slap them on with enthusiasm. POR15 doesn't wash off skin, though, so time your use of it to avoid going to any smart events.

The other area where there have been notable improve-

ments is in sound deadening. This came about in a big way during the 1990s' fascination for huge automotive sound systems, a fashion that has to some extent come and gone. Part of that involved controlling noise levels inside cars, and stopping thin steel panels reverberating and vibrating. My friend Mad Frank from Belgium had one of the loudest Minivans in Europe, and the speakers literally blew the roof off it when vibration cracked the seam along the roof panel. The adhesive sound-deadening mat that would have stopped this happening is excellent stuff and very effective in reducing what's now known as 'NVH' (noise, vibration, harshness) levels in old cars that never had any padding at all other than carpets.

When it comes to carpets, we are well served nowadays. I've always liked Coverdale's workmanship, and they cover all our models of Triumph. Currently a set of their man-made and therefore convertible-appropriate ordinary carpets for a Spitfire costs £134, and for the more waterproof Triumphs such as a Vitesse saloon, you can opt for 80 per cent wool at £205 and full luxury wool at £266. With sound-deadening mat fitted to a solid shell and good thick wool carpets, a Vitesse in 2016 will be an even more pleasant environment that it was in 1969.

STEERING WHEELS AND WOODWORK

The steering wheel is one of your main points of contact with controlling the car, and is also a centrepiece of the interior. The standard Triumph wheels are usually rather nice, but there are plenty of improvements on offer. Anything from Moto-Lita or Nardi will look good and will feel very good, although it's a mistake to combine a smaller steering wheel with bigger tyres if you plan to do any parking. Larger steering wheels offer much more leverage and therefore much lighter steering. While all rally enthusiasts and spectators in the 1970s used tiny steering wheels at arm's length, those actually driving rally cars used big and deeply dished wheels so that they could use their shoulders and feel what was going on with the front wheels. In the absence of power steering, the same still applies.

Dynamat is a modern technology sound-reduction mat and works very effectively on old cars in reducing noise, vibration and harshness. You get to listen to the exhaust note instead.
R. LAMBRECHT

It's not particularly easy to match woods between dashboards and steering wheels, but by stripping both and then applying a common stain, you can get close. Darker wood colours will help.

One unpleasant but common mistake is mismatching colours of woods between the wheel and the dashboard. Even Rolls-Royce did this, with an optional Nardi wheel on 1970s Corniches that clashed unpleasantly with the completely differently coloured burr-walnut dashboard.

Both the dash and the steering wheel rims can be chemically stripped and then stained the same colour, with more layers of stain used to darken the lighter of the two woods. With enough varnish this can look glorious. Moto-Lita supplies wheels with no colour or varnish, on request.

Canadian GT8 (5.0 Ford engine) has quite a nice woodrim wheel, but the dashboard varnish is flaking off. Time for a total woodwork sort-out, with the dash stained to match the wheel.

Vitesse and Herald interiors became quite attractive after the first few years. No leather, but with a fair amount of woodwork. A formula woodrim steering wheel seems to have been a very common option.

Later Spitfire interiors became more plush and comfy as the years went on. Final 1500cc cars were more tourers than sports cars. P. BARLOW

If your dash veneer is cracked anyway, here's your chance to transform the interior by matching the new veneer to the colour of the steering-wheel rim. All the wooden surfaces inside Triumphs are simple and virtually flat, so applying new veneer is within the capabilities of all of us. The veneer can be bought quite cheaply – locally to me, the hobby supply shop offers wood veneers that are treated to avoid cracking, and which are $^{1}/_{100}$in thick, and 24in (61cm) wide by 96in (244cm) long. The choice is between mahogany, cherry, red or white oak, maple or walnut, and the price is about £30. That's enough acreage to do a complete Vitesse dashboard and door

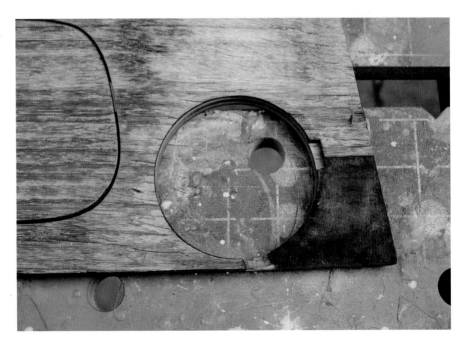

With flat dashboards, it's relatively easy to strip the old veneer off and glue on some new, and it's not too expensive.

tops, including making a mess of it and doing it again. Match the unstained veneer as closely as you can to the unstained plywood steering-wheel wood, and then use the same stain and many coats of oil-based yacht varnish. Old wood-rim steering wheels can also be rescued cheaply, stripped, re-stained and re-varnished.

INSTRUMENTS

Smiths Instruments, or rather the Speedy Cables section of Smiths Instruments, can still refurbish original Triumph instruments, and in some cases can still supply them new. Many of their Classic instrument range are standard

This is my Mini dash, re-veneered in supposedly sustainable African red mahogany veneer and then a few coats of varnish. Acceptable for a home job, although more coats would have been better.

Finally a seriously nice interior, with leather and deeply, richly varnished wood, and with the wheel matched to the dash in colour and tone. In a Gentry Triumph-based kit car. R. HAWKINS

Auto Meter sells good, plain, easy-to-read instruments with hi-viz orange needles, for reasonable prices. Real Steel in Uxbridge market them in the UK.

If you're serious about going quickly and tend to get carried away, this Auto Meter tacho tells you whether or not you've over-revved the engine, and if so, how badly. Mind you, so does a bent valve.

period instruments for the Triumphs of the period (www. caigauge.com). The company can also convert original tachometers to read pulses rather than using cables, for those updating to more modern ignition and fuelling.

Good value and accurate readings are offered by the American company Auto Meter, whose plainer offerings with large dials and orange needles give you an instant engine health check with a glance across the needles. They have some amusing automotive jewellery as well in their more fashionable ranges of dashboard entertainment, with coloured back lighting, electronic widgetry and drag-racing tachometers with many functions.

Changing to a completely new set of instruments is a bit daunting, but at least everything is new and makes a good connection. Make sure fuel gauges and senders are matched for resistance.

9 electrics

THE ANATOMY OF A WIRING LOOM

To make sense of the wiring loom, first find the fuseboxes. This is the beginning of a generic Lucas-based wiring loom supplied for my Triumph Midge kit car.

Next are the connections for the hazard warning unit and the flasher unit.

The blue multi-plug is the connection for the front wiring loom that goes to the lights and other peripheral items.

The two orange multi-plugs are for the rear end of the peripheral loom.

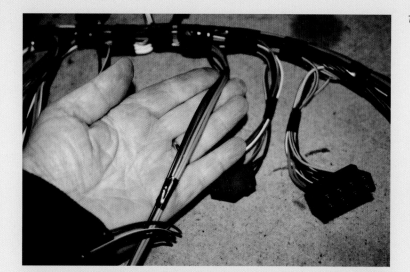

This branch goes to the wiper motor.

The next branch goes to the reversing light switch – cut the wires short, tape over the ends and tape the wires into the main bundle of the loom if you don't have reversing lights.

Next is the plug for the dashboard connections.

Green and yellow wires go off to the heater blower motor.

This bundle of paired wires goes to the various dash-mounted warning lights.

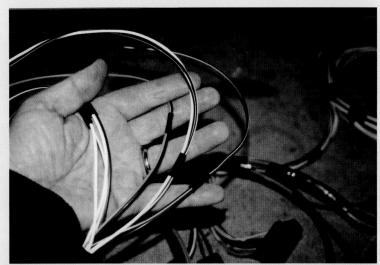

The next little bundle is for the switch for the hazard lights, well worth wiring in if you don't currently have any.

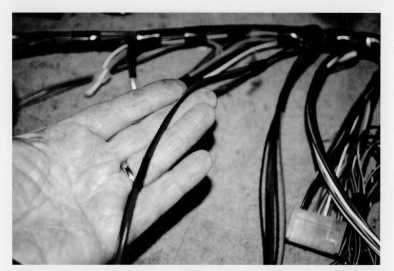

Another optional extra – the rear high intensity fog light. For old cars they're still optional.

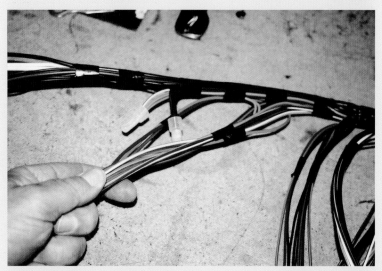

The column switchgear is next – one area where the Midge could do with the wiring trimmed a little, so that it's somewhere near the right length rather than hanging down like a bunch of grapes.

This is the earth wire for the dashboard: it's crucial for the earth wires to be attached to clean, shiny steel on the chassis or body.

Red and white goes to the ignition switch. Even I knew that.

The white block is the multi-plug for accessories.

The next pair of wires, still in the dash area, goes to the brake-light switch on the pedal. The instrument loom looks imposing, but there aren't really that many wires. Just change like for like to replicate the original loom.

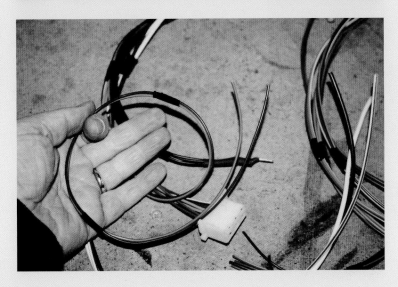

The front loom goes to the peripherals. The main loom remains inside the cabin.

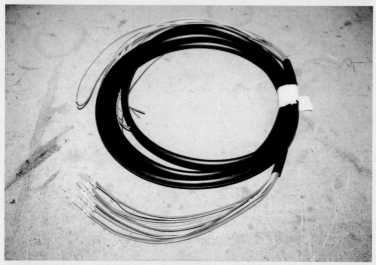

The back loom is split into two – most of the electrical action is under the dashboard, so the rearward wiring has further to go.

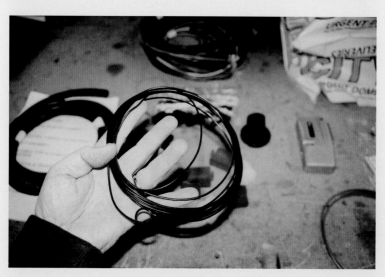

The black wire is for earthing. Bad earths cause many wiring hassles with old cars, so make sure contact points are clean, shiny steel, and then apply paint to seal the connection from damp. This loom came from www.premierwiring.co.uk.

This is your package from Premier, with enough spare wire to reach to both ends of any kit car. It looks like multi-coloured spaghetti, but makes sense quite quickly.

EARTHING

The ghost of Joseph Lucas, the inventor of darkness, has been blamed for suspect electrics on old British cars for almost a century now, but much of this is unfair. There is quiet pleasure to be taken in watching people poking through boxes of autojumble crap in 2016 searching for genuine Lucas parts.

The cause of sudden darkness in a very high percentage of instances is not usually the influence of the ghost of Joseph Lucas, but the more prosaic one of bad earths or grounds. I once had to drive my Vitesse from Grantham to London with the only available frontal lighting being the main-beam flasher, due to rust and a bad earth.

To get a really good earth, clean, bare metal contacts must be firmly attached to clean, bare metal bodywork or chassis, and the resulting union must be protected by either dielectric grease or preferably paint. In reality, a contact on a British car will have been attached in 1965 with a machine screw, and even if it still looks all right, the contact will be invisibly corroded to some extent. When the contact gets bad enough, electricity will turn to heat or will amble off elsewhere in search of an easier earth, which could be through another bulb, or a horn, or a doomed light switch that is being used as a ten-year slow-blow fuse.

Incidentally, Mr Lucas can certainly take the blame for designing headlamp circuits with no fuse and no relay: if left like that, the headlamp circuit and switch must be regarded as temporary, and planning to get home every day before dark would be prudent. Putting a relay into the circuit takes most of the load off the original switch, which then just directs rather than carries the main current. It should then last indefinitely.

Useful goodies in the bag include trunking, grommets, a wire stripper and crimper, and even some tie-wraps.

ELECTRIC FANS

Electric fans are becoming more necessary every year as the roads become increasingly congested with ever more cars. The official government estimate of the British population is probably wrong by 30 per cent, based on Tesco's grocery sales figures. Large-scale immigration of youth and energy brings benefits as well as problems, but one downside is that the traffic in the UK is only ever going to get worse. Heralds and Spitfires were designed in a country with a population of half the current number, in the year when the first few miles of the amazing new M1 motorway were opened. They were designed for ambling along A roads at 50 and 60mph (80 and 100km/h), and not for being driven for several hours at 70mph (110km/h) on a motorway, or crawling for several hours at walking pace on the same motorway, depending on luck. There's also fifty years of collected crud deposits in the coolant galleries in the cylinder block.

Electric fans are more efficient than engine-mounted fans. They're also quieter, they let the engine warm up faster, and they save petrol: you'll be getting the drift of my thinking on fans by now. They should replace the now redundant mechanical engine fan, which wastes a lot of fuel, they should be behind the radiator and pulling air through it, they should be fused, and they should have an override switch – you know your car and how it behaves in traffic, and you should be able to switch it on when the temperature gauge makes you nervous. The automatic temperature switch is operated by a sensor that must be mounted low in the water system, probably in the lower rad hose, as it can't read the temperature of steam and will tell you that the engine is cold when it's seriously overheating.

REPLACE THE FUSEBOX AND FUSES

In relation to earthing, there is absolutely no excuse not to replace the fusebox and fuses: these cost next to nothing, and if all the contacts are fresh and clean, you have just either repaired or prevented an assortment of electrical failures. Even if an old fusebox looks good, its metal surfaces will have been superficially corroding for decades.

The new blade fuses may or may not be better at conducting current: a more usual reason for design and manufacturing changes in fuses is that the new type are going to be a lot cheaper to manufacture than glass tubes with wire and end caps. Looking at the design, though, they do make a better contact than a weak spring clip as on the old fuseboxes, as this couldn't be made too strong or it would break the glass. The main advantage of changing to blade fuses is that you can get them wherever there is a Halfords or a garage. If you stick with authentic glass fuses, they should be bought in quantity at classic car shows when you get the chance, because their availability is decreasing annually at a compound rate.

Where wiring passes through a bulkhead, the sharp steel edge would soon cut through the wires, cause a dead short and start a fire, so grommets are used to protect them.

Whether you use a posh or a cheap wire crimper, it's a much better way of stripping wire ends and clamping on spade connectors than using your teeth.

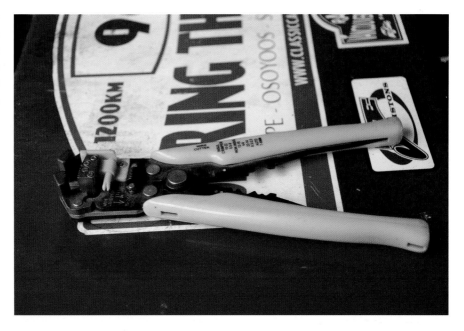

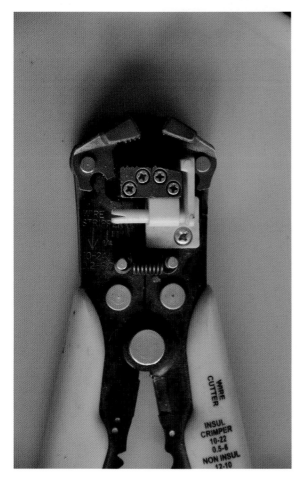

ADDING A HAZARD CIRCUIT

For an almost free, emergency-only system, you can use a switch to bridge the wires going to the indicator bulbs after the existing flasher unit. However, that is for emergencies only, as it carries risks: it would double the current going through old components, it would overload a flasher unit not designed to operate four bulbs, and you would have to leave the ignition on to get current to the flasher, which means you would have to disconnect the low tension wire to the coil. If the points are closed and the circuit is live, the coil and/or condenser will burn out, which leaves you even more broken down than you were when you switched the hazard lights on. On the up side, if the car is on fire, the RAC won't have any trouble finding it.

This bodgery can be slightly ameliorated by upgrading to a bigger flasher unit designed to work four bulbs, which means just about all recent ones. To do the job properly, you need a replica of the Lucas SB300 kit, which is specifically a retro-fitting kit for adding four-way flashers to older cars. Holden stocks them. If you do that, you can then use them regularly, as van drivers do, to alert other drivers that you've parked somewhere stupid.

The posh crimper strips half an inch (a centimetre) or so of plastic from the end of the wire without damaging any of the copper strands.

ALTERNATORS: AN UPGRADE?

Upgrading to an alternator is not a foregone conclusion. Alternators are more powerful and more reliable than dynamos, but they are more complex and cannot be fettled by the roadside. My Vitesse-based Midge retains its dynamo and control box and it usually works just fine. A Triumph in regular use in queueing winter commuter traffic would probably benefit from an alternator conversion, as a dynamo could well struggle to power headlights, wipers and the heater fan from the smaller amount of current generated at low rpm by an idling engine.

Dynamos have a commutator spinning inside a ring, and carbon brushes conduct current to a control box, which uses sprung contacts to control the amount of current sent to the battery. Stuck brushes can be unstuck

An alternator is visibly a newer generation of electricity generator. This owner has tried to distract your attention from the anachronistic alternator by wrapping wires in very colourful protective wrapping. Did it work?

The splendid and helpful late British car designer William Towns once told me that if you don't like something on a car, paint it black. A small alternator painted black does disappear unless you cruelly light it and point a camera at it.

The diode pack in an alternator is what eventually fails and needs to be replaced. Alternators are more easily available, more powerful and more efficient, though.

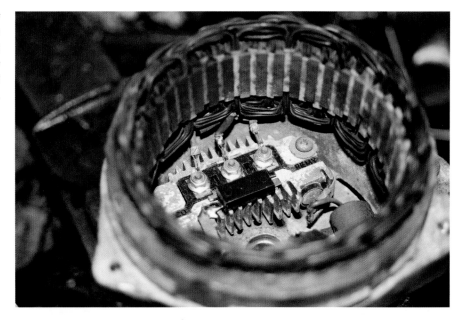

Dynamos are much slimmer than alternators and work well enough, and my bonnet side won't shut on an alternator anyway. The dynamo stays, then.

or replaced, corroded or burnt contacts can be scraped and adjusted, and you can be on your way after a push start.

Alternators work basically the same way, but current adjustments are controlled by electronic diodes. These do fail in the end, and as already mentioned, alternators cannot be fettled at the roadside. The diodes can, however, be replaced cheaply by being soldered in, and they

only cost £20 or so – so it wouldn't be a bad idea to acquire a spare set to keep in your main toolbox.

HIGH-TORQUE GEARED STARTER MOTORS

In the same way that alternators are a progressive and conceptual improvement over dynamos, modern high-torque, geared starter motors are an improvement over old Lucas starters. A universal NipponDenso starter motor is mounted on a ring that attaches the motor to various engines, and as supplied, the starter motor may not fit at all. The mounting ring has to be removed and spun round so that the mounting bolts line up where the Triumph starter motor was mounted. The ring is then bolted back on and the starter will fit. Some bolts may need to be shortened if the mounting is too shallow.

BRIGHTER HEADLIGHTS

Ordinary sealed beam headlights fitted to most period British cars are in the 55/60 watt bracket. The bulb structure is the same as an old-school house bulb – a filament glowing in a vacuum and, with no oxygen available, it doesn't burn up. If you want brighter headlights, a tungsten-halogen conversion kit is the usual route. The sealed beam unit is effectively a big bulb with its own lens, while a halogen headlight tends to be a glass-fronted reflector that carries a separate bulb, which has a tungsten filament and is filled with halogen gas. Lucas H4 halogen bulbs can be bought in the same wattage but give more and whiter light, or you can choose to buy more powerful bulbs.

The downside of that is that the current still runs though the unfused light switch, which should be regarded as a slow-blow fuse. It will blow or melt more quickly if it has to deal with more current from brighter bulbs, so adding relays is the way to go. Extra 'driving' lamps are actually illegal: they are a nuisance for everybody coming the other way, and there isn't really anywhere on either a Herald/Vitesse or a Spitfire/GT6 that you can fit additional lamps where they would look good, apart from possibly a pair of Lucas fog/spots on an early Herald with the recessed radiator grille.

WIRING LOOMS

A while back, the wiring on my ancient Midge began to look decidedly nasty, so it was time to consider the options. The Midge chassis is basically a ladder in thick steel, which helps with earthing. The original Triumph wiring loom was recycled into the new body just as it had come out of the donor Vitesse, having been chopped about slightly to get it to more or less the right length, and it was then taped up and secured to the bodywork with lots of clips. It lasted well: the only major electrical issue was a burnt-out dynamo that took the regulator box out with it, and there has been some fiddling with earths and switches to keep all the peripheral lights and so on working. No problems, really.

The original wiring around the steering column worked well enough, but was rather a mess. The old bullet connectors work well as long as they're not rusty inside – but after thirty-three years they do tend to be corroded, so it's best to replace them.

It did, however, start to look very tired and dirty, so it was time to check out the options for replacing it. The good news is that the options are much cheaper and easier than they used to be: you can mix and match modern and original equipment as much as you like, and just suit yourself. For example, on a Midge one can hardly claim to be too bothered about originality, but changing from the old dynamo and regulator box to a modern alternator generates, as it were, a Midge-specific problem: the alternators are too fat and the narrow bonnet won't shut on one. There was already a box on the other side of the bonnet where the carbs stuck out, so I didn't want another lump on the nearside.

I used Premier Wiring's Uniloom intended for kit cars, which is still based on the sort of simple looms that powered Spitfires and Minis, and is still sold in Lucas colours. The copper of the new wire is either the same as, or thicker than, the original, but the exterior PVC coating is thinner and lighter. Premier's Alan Boxall used to make pre-cut looms for specific cars, but he ended up with dozens of huge sheets of plywood, covered in nails and looking like model railway layouts, on which he made up the looms. Making many different looms took a lot of time as well, and was inevitably expensive. He changed his approach, gambling on the idea that people would probably prefer to pay a lot less for a universal generic old-Brit wiring loom and to trim the peripheral wires themselves. He was right – we do. However, advice over the phone is included in the price of each loom, and he will still help out with special requirements.

You can stay fairly close to the original spec of your car. If you want to keep the wiring looking right, you can retain the dynamo, the regulator box and the old-style fusebox with glass fuses. The wires for the electric fan, fog light, reversing light and so on are included in the new loom, but if you don't want those functions, you either cut those wires off, or just tape them off and don't use them.

For a more practical car to tour with rather than to fiddle with, Premier's Uniloom has all the bits you need for a major electrical update or a complete new wiring job, including wires for a fan and an alternator. You can also choose to redesign where things are – so if you fancy a fusebox kept dry and immediately available inside the glove box, that's up to you.

Adding an electric fan is easy. The wiring is now there, so you just need to mount and power up the fan, fit the sensor in the bottom hose, and take off the old mechanical fan completely.

The looms are supplied with all the wires far too long, so the idea is that you make up the loom on a table to your own measurements, or ideally with the old loom alongside to duplicate it accurately, and simply cut off and discard what you don't need. Measure twice, cut once, as ever. There's a crimping tool included free in the kit, together with all the connections you need, and a new fusebox too, as well as new trunking and critically important bulkhead grommets to avoid the loom chafing on the edges of the holes in the body and setting fire to the car.

The large bag of wire does look daunting when it arrives, but you simply start at one end and identify a tail-light wire. Then do the other side. By the time you've identified all the bits and got to the other end, the loom will make sense. Putting it back into the car also looks as though it could be horribly complicated, but each

Mini restoration expert Martin Webber works with similar BL Lucas looms to Triumphs, and is quite happy to clean old ones up and refresh the contacts: but if he spots any Scotchlocks or bodging, the loom goes straight in the bin. This is useful and hard-won knowledge.

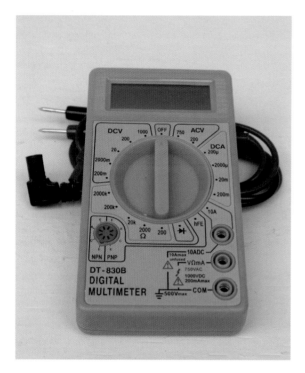

Multimeters are very useful for establishing where current is or, more importantly, isn't going, and are now more or less the same price as a bit of wire and a bulb.

FOG AND BRAKE LIGHTS

A rear fog light, or a pair of rear fog lights, has to be a good idea. You don't need them legally for nearly all the Triumphs of our period because they are only required from 1981, but used creatively, they make a lot of sense. A couple of suggestions, though: they look very unprofessional just hanging off the rear bumper. They can be slung right under the car – they only need to be seen by cars behind you, so they can be hung from the boot floor behind the rear valance and will be just visible from behind. I would also wire them to light up with the brake lights. The third brake lights fitted to newer cars will have worked for a while, but are becoming ineffective as everybody gets used to them. If you have four bright brake lights operating, that might just stop some careless punter from rear-ending you, and if you have standard Triumph seats with no head restraints, that has to be a smart move. You can also wire the fog lights to be turned on permanently if it's actually foggy, and also if somebody's tailgating you at night.

BATTERY CUT-OFF SWITCHES

For racing, one of the basic scrutineering requirements for car preparation is a visible and marked battery cut-off switch, so that track marshals can turn off the current on a crashed car and reduce the fire risk – although oddly enough, according to a fireman I was chatting to, flammable brake fluid is now much more of a fire risk than unleaded fuel.

Be that as it may, the cut-off switches are usually simple affairs, quite often with a detachable plastic key. If you run a longer main power cable through the bulkhead via a grommet and mount such a switch on the cable under the dash, you can take the key when you leave the car, and stealing it will immediately become much harder. You can also opt for a simpler switch on the top of the battery positive terminal, of the type that unscrews. If your bonnet is fitted with locks, which nowadays it probably should be, again it makes stealing the car a much longer and more difficult process.

Some cut-off switches have little cables that allow enough current to maintain settings on stereo head units.

Another advantage is that if you have a current leak somewhere in the car but have disconnected the battery completely with a switch, the fault can't run the battery flat and kill it if the car is unused for a while. Trickle or maintenance-charging the battery is always wise anyway, and the battery doesn't need to be electrically connected to the car to be charged.

wire you identify and connect leaves one less to worry about, and before you know it, the new loom is finished. Fitting a shiny new loom is in many ways much easier than getting tired old electrics to play the game. I've just finished a book on Mini restoration, and one interesting thing to note was that my technical editor, who ran a Mini garage for twelve years on his own and had to cope with all aspects of old British cars, had a strict rule about old wiring looms. If they were just dirty and corroded, he would refresh and repair them; but if he saw any Scotchloks or other evidence of amateur butchery, he would rip the whole lot out and fit a new loom. That's probably a good rule.

Earthing is crucial, so make sure that any black earth wires are solidly connected to shiny clean metal.

I know that some people regard wiring as a horrible bogey that they wouldn't touch with somebody else's bargepole, but it's really not too complicated when you just get on with it. Mind you, electricity does sometimes regard the laws of physics more as suggestions than laws as such, and it doesn't always comply unless it's in the right mood.

You can't lose the key for a rotary battery cut-off switch, but with an unlockable bonnet, it doesn't add much security. It does stop battery drain during lay-ups, though.

LED BULBS

Having LED bulbs only really applies to secondary lighting such as side-, tail- and indicator lights; it's possible to have 7in LED headlights, but they're very expensive and rather tarty, and they would look rubbish on a classic car. LED sidelight and brake-light bulbs are a lot brighter than conventional filament bulbs, they use almost no current and generate no heat, and they last well too. The downside is that they don't use enough current to operate the standard flasher unit, so you need a matching LED-ready flasher unit to work with LED indicator bulbs.

HEATER IMPROVEMENTS

The first step to better heating is to check that the thermostat and radiator pressure caps are working properly, and probably to replace them. If you can't find a good quality, expensive example of either, buy additional cheap ones to be sure you've got one that works.

The heater is a radiator, nothing more or less than a smaller replica of the main rad. It's likely that the main radiator or core has been replaced in the last fifty years,

The extra lights on later pre-facelift Spitfires do look like afterthoughts, because that's what they are. Safety is a consideration, though – earlier less-lit Spits are prettier but more likely to be rear-ended.

The Karmann redesign didn't result in the usual howl of protest from people who don't like change, because it was somewhere between just as pretty and an improvement. Bigger, safer lights are a bonus.

but it's also quite likely that the heater core has not. If they're thoroughly plugged up with decades of filth, they quite often don't leak, but nor do they do anything else much in the way of providing any heating either. When back-flushed and chemically cleaned, they often then spray out water like a fountain because the detritus that previously plugged all the pinholes has been cleaned away.

Once the core has been replaced, make an effort to seal any gaps between the heater core and the outer casing with foam plastic and discreetly applied metal duct tape – actual duct tape is useless for ducting, which is what we're doing – to seal off any air leaks so that all incoming air is directed through the tubing and vanes of the heater core. With the heater working even better than originally designed, next winter's driving will be toasty.

IN CONCLUSION

To close this chapter, here's a nice new American Lucas-inspired joke:

Why don't the British make televisions?

Because they haven't yet figured out how to make them leak oil.

Electricity is smoke. When the smoke has got out of the wires, Lucas have thoughtfully provided us with replacement smoke. The smoke insertion tool is no longer available, sadly, so it must now be done by hand.

Earthing or grounding isn't a big problem in San Diego with freshly restored cars and no rain to speak of, but it is for most of us. Lights and other electricals must be earthed to solid metal and then the contact sealed with paint or dielectric grease.

10

maintaining performance

The most useful thing you can do regarding maintenance on a 6-cylinder Triumph is to keep your foot off the clutch pedal, which will avoid terminal, or at best very expensive, wear of the rear of the crankcase.

Other than that, getting the engine set up properly and keeping it in tune will make the most of any improvements you've achieved. It's worth the admittedly rather fearsome expense of a rolling road session for initially setting up the carburation and ignition to be as good as it can be, and to correct any mistakes and mismatches of performance goodies that might have been made. I have run many dyno shootouts for performance magazines, and have had to maintain a tactfully straight face as many people discover to their horror, and soundtracked by the derisive hooting of their unsympathetic friends, that the vast amounts of money they have thrown into shiny performance catalogue temptations have reduced the performance of their engines to below bog-standard.

You need to get the basics properly sorted out. Getting the right needles and jets in a carburettor and making

sure the bobweights in a mechanical distributor are functioning correctly could yield significantly more bhp than a porting job and an extra carb. The best possible settings for timing and fuel on your particular engine are best achieved on a rolling road, but those default settings remain correct from then on, unless something changes.

Electronic ignition is only a benefit until it fails, and its failure rate in my cars is 100 per cent. The wise Triumph enthusiast will have retained the original points and condenser or the whole distributor in a box in the boot for just such an eventuality. Points are simple and reliable, and they require cleaning and adjusting every 1,500 miles (2,500km) or so. If they're clean they will last well, if dirty less so, as dirty points tend to burn out faster. With the extremely convenient flip front on our Triumphs, you can sit on a front wheel while sorting out the points. If that's still too much hassle, you can replace the actual points themselves with an optical switch. This doesn't involve any complex electronics, and just replaces the distributor cam lobes with a 'chopper', looking rather like a radiator fan,

Theoretically, replacing the points with an electronic system or a Hall-effect switch makes your car more reliable. This is true, until it packs up. Keep a spare mechanical distributor or a set of spare points and a condenser in the boot.

The lump on the distributor shaft is a cam that opens up the ignition points, and then lets them close to send a spark to the plug. The condenser is a voltage spike absorber. Keeping it that simple just means adjusting the points, and replacing them and the condenser annually.

that spins inside the distributor and alternately obscures and reveals a light beam that makes and breaks contact in the same way that the points did. Such a switch is also less affected by wear in the distributor: if the shaft or cam lobes in a points-based distributor are worn, the points gap won't be very consistent.

Collecting spares in the distributor department is worthwhile: a persistent misfire in my last MGB was finally sorted with the third new distributor, so spare ones that are known to be working should be treasured, and at least one should be kept in the back of your car. Rotors and distributor caps should be changed annually, although good plug leads should last a while.

PETROL AND OIL

Life with an old Triumph is not as simple as it once was, as the fluids involved have changed. Fuel is now mixed with ethanol, a biofuel that damages seals and hoses made from older materials. Ethanol is ethically dubious, as it occupies fields that could be growing food, but that's another issue. From our point of view, the decision about rebuilding or not rebuilding older carbs has been taken on our behalf. Ethanol and other new petrol chemicals are unavoidable and can destroy some older carb manufacturing materials that were previously adequate, so unless our carbs have been fairly recently rebuilt, we need to fit new seals, flexible hoses and sometimes floats to avoid fuel leaks and possibly a fire.

The removal of lead from fuel also means that its lubrication qualities have been lost, and every time a steel valve opens and closes on a plain cast-iron valve seat it micro-welds itself to the seat, and tears out a tiny piece of the cylinder head. Over a few years, this erosion will eventually remove enough material to stop the valve sealing, and at that point the engine will become difficult to start. A hardened valve seat then needs to be fitted, which permanently solves the problem. Triumph cylinder-head iron is fairly hard, so Triumph heads last quite well: there is

no rush to carry out this procedure, and no harm is being done by continuing to drive the car, other than to an area of the head that will be milled out anyway and will end up as swarf on an engineering shop's floor.

Oil additive composition is also posing a problem these days. Because of catalytic convertors and emission, the levels of ZDDP, a zinc compound, have been reduced back to 1950s levels. That's okay, then, you might think: our cars have 1950s engines. True, but engines in the 1950s were only expected to last for 30,000 miles (48,300km) between rebuilds. A major problem is the friction between the rocker tips and the valves, where one surface drags across the other. There isn't enough zinc in modern oil to lubricate that. You can choose to fit roller rockers and then use modern low-zinc oil, but modern oils are also much thinner and designed for newer engines with much closer engineering tolerances, and you can run into low oil-pressure problems with oil that's too runny.

A classic 20/50 such as Miller's will do the job, the American equivalent being Kendall GT-1 racing oil. The mileage between oil and filter changes is 3,000 miles

Millers Oils have always proved an unbiased, reliable and knowledgeable source of information to me as a journalist, and they know whereof they speak: I would happily use their Classic 20/50 in a Triumph engine.

Importing British oil across the Atlantic is expensive, so we use Kendall GT-1 racing 20/50 oil, which has plenty of zinc in it and is actually cheaper than mainstream modern oils, a bonus.

(4,800km). Trunnions, dashpots and other fluid or semi-fluid levels should be checked at the same time.

Oil filters have also changed, mostly for the better. A remote spin-on cartridge filter system is best, and also most convenient. While the old-school Triumph oil-filter housing unbolts with a spanner, the spin-on type is undone by hand. It should be hand tight, but if it's too tight to unscrew easily, you will generally find some yellow rubber gloves under your sink that are ideal for getting a grip on the filter – though don't get caught using them for this job. Filters for Triumphs should also have non-return flaps in them in order to stop all the oil

The spares box in the back of my car contains last year's distributor cap and leads, rotor, plugs and points, and a couple of condensers that I know are working, as well as a spare coil, which again I know works.

In a 1991 magazine article, I recommended a very similar box of spares, carried aboard the Ayrspeed XK120 replica I manufactured and used as a daily driver. NOS Lucas parts weren't treasured back then, they were complained about.

draining back down to the sump, otherwise the noise you hear on starting a cold engine is the big ends banging, which will go on until the oil pump has filled up the oil filter and then finally got around to sending some oil to the moving parts.

Incidentally, the plug on the head that looks as though it might be for an extra oil feed pipe is not – it's a hole left over from the casting process. If you fit an extra oil pipe to it you will be adding an unnecessary extra oil supply to cheap rocker parts and at the same time starving expensive crankshaft parts of oil. As you can imagine, this is a notably unwise decision.

The oils in the gearbox and differential need to be changed every few years, along with the brake fluid. The gear parts are frankly inadequate and have a hard life, and when you change their oil you are maintaining the oil viscosity and condition as well as you can, and you are also draining out metallic swarf generated by wear and tear. Metal swarf is better out than in.

Brake fluid also needs changing every couple of years, because it is hygroscopic and attracts water from the atmosphere. That water collects at the lowest part of the system, which is the wheel cylinders, which is why they in turn corrode, rip up the seals and start leaking. Biennial fluid changes will help reduce this.

TRUNNION NOISE

The front suspension trunnions on Triumphs don't make any noises themselves other than the bang when they fail if they're not lubricated. Fortunately this frequently happens at parking speeds when taking advantage of the absurd turning circle of the smaller Triumphs. However, sometimes it doesn't happen at parking speeds, so maintenance is fairly important. The question is, with what, and there has been a huge amount of discussion, previously in saloon bars and latterly on the Internet, about whether they should be lubricated with oil or with grease.

The most important thing is that they must be lubricated one way or the other, and frequently. Triumph recommended oil, the theory behind this being that there is contact between bronze and steel, resulting in the creation of bronze fragments. The refreshing of the oil supposedly washes out this swarf, whereas swarf-laden grease can supposedly cake and jam. Many grease-based Internetters have greased their trunnions for decades and have had no problem, as likewise have many oil-based Internetters. But the point is, they have all lubricated their trunnions religiously, which is undoubtedly a lot more important than the viscosity of the lubricant used. The TSSC sells an oil gun specifically for the trunnions, so putting that on the Christmas present list has to be a smart move. The favourite seems to be 90-weight oil, as used in the gearbox and diff.

The points are set at 0.015in, or fifteen-thousandths of an inch, and the spark-plug gap is 0.025in. The gap is measured by feeling slight resistance when sliding the (squeaky clean, not oily) feeler gauge through the relevant gap.

My screwdriver drawer is a random collection of variable quality: if you're tooling up for the first time, it is better to get a few good ones, and don't lend them to anybody.

STORAGE

Many people store their classics over the winter, although they rust just as fast in the summer. If that's the way you like to roll, it's still best if you can keep the car mobile and take it out for a 10-mile (16km) run fairly regularly; there are always a few crisp, crystal-clear sunny days in midwinter that make this a pleasure. Don't just start the engine briefly every so often, as this invites condensation and corrosion. If you can't drive the car but do want to start the engine, run it up to full operating temperature before turning it off.

Because of the ethanol in fuel, which also attracts water and causes corrosion, a car that is to be laid up for a while should have fuel stabilizer added to the fuel in the tank, and should be kept with the tank either full, or drained and completely empty.

Constantly charging the battery with an automatic top-up charger is a good idea, but get a good one – some of the cheap ones don't work very well.

Before putting the car away, it's also worth touching in any paint chips to stop rust creeping under the paint. To keep the interior in good shape, use some dessicant bags to keep the humidity down. Leaving the windows open a crack works well, but it also invites small squatters in the form of rats and mice. Rodents don't require a court order for eviction, but they are nonetheless extremely bad tenants.

Obviously if you live where salt is used on the roads, a pressure wash underneath is wise before a winter lay-up. A nut and bolt check before springtime awakening is wise, and torquing the wheel nuts before (and after) any cheeky driving is wise: they must be checked every hour during track days as they will regularly come loose.

Tyres don't tend to develop flat spots over just a few months of standing still, although it would be wise to leave more, rather than less, pressure in them. Taking the weight off them altogether by putting the car on axle stands definitely avoids any possible flat spots, and keeping the wheels and tyres in the dark and somewhere completely different will both extend the life of the rubber and also make it very difficult to steal the car. Tyres in regular use and not protected from ultraviolet light last about seven years before becoming too hard to be safe.

Leave the handbrake off to avoid the back brakes seizing on, and operate the clutch pedal whenever you visit the car, to discourage the clutch from sticking to the flywheel.

The same applies to pliers – fewer and of better quality would be better than a drawerful of tools, some of which were found in the back of secondhand Triumphs in the 1970s.

Here's an example of actual progress, rather than stuff just getting cheaper and nastier. Ratchet spanners used to be an expensive luxury, but now Halfords' well regarded Professional range can be had for £40 for a good set.

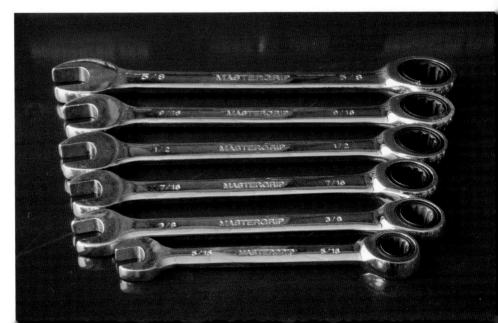

BARN FINDS

Barn finds are weirdly popular nowadays, to the extent that there was semi-humorous talk locally in Vancouver of giving a hard-to-sell Alvis a 'patina' of pigeon droppings and dust, and 'finding' it in a barn. However, in active pottering around the world of classic cars, you might well find yourself wanting to recommission a car after a long period of slumber. If the body and chassis are good enough to make it worthwhile, if the price is right, and if you have turned the engine a complete revolution with a spanner on the crankshaft, you're in business. However, recommissioning a long-unused car is likely to require the following:

♦ New brake and clutch lines and hoses
♦ Rebuild or replacement of master and slave cylinders
♦ New tyres
♦ A rebuilt or replaced fuel system from tank to carb
♦ A cooling system overhaul, unless the car has been left with no fluids in it

On the up side, when a discovered rescued car is aroused from many years of coma and fires up into life again, amidst smoke, clatterings and grubby grins – that moment is what it's all about.

If you're planning to spend significant time playing about with old cars, it's worth doing the sums on air tools versus electric tools. Compressor power claims are frequently dishonest nonsense, though. What you need for power tools up to a small orbital sander is a genuine 15cfm (cubic feet per minute) at 90psi (pounds per square inch).

On the up side, a set like this with powerful and industrial-quality air tools could be bought for a great deal less than the electric equivalent, and air tools are tougher, more powerful, and pose no fire risk.

A good 2-litre GT6 is a nicely balanced little car, so it was astonishing to find that a 5-litre V8 made it even more civilized – although instant monster was on offer as well.

11

case studies

Improving a Triumph for a reasonable budget using a few weekend hours is rewarding and absorbing, but the options range from sharpening up the performance and handling of a fairly standard car to complete changes of bodywork and drivetrain.

If you have no experience of spanners it is probably wise to start off with repairing and uprating an existing usable car – but it might be worth knowing that I was an advertising copywriter when I built the Midge featured below, and I built it in a small Ealing garage with no electricity. I wouldn't say it was easy, or that the resulting car was show quality, but it got done and it was fun.

Below are a few examples of other Triumph enthusiasts who have come up with a variety of approaches and outcomes.

RON LAMBRECHT'S SPIT 6

For many people, the unofficially named Spit 6 is the ultimate small Triumph. It's a Spitfire body with a GT6 chas-

sis and running gear, which brings with it a variety of other GT6 mechanical upgrades compared to the Spitfire mechanicals. The Spit 6 is lighter but not as well balanced as a GT6: with the heavy six fitted, it's faster but slightly more unruly with its lighter back end. Many people like that combination, and of course it's convertible.

Ron Lambrecht lives in San Diego, and contrary to the expectations of hardtop Brits, driving around with the roof off is actually more fun in reasonable British temperatures than in really high California temperatures. It is indeed lovely looking at the brilliant sunshine, palm trees and azure ocean, but it's better to look out at it from the shade than to be dazzled and baked. Ron has the perfect combination – his white hardtop reflects the serious heat of the midday SoCal sun, and it can also be taken off during the evening or on cooler days.

Ron's car is a 1970 GT6 with a 1970 Spitfire body and a 2-litre engine that is mildly hot-rodded with the head skimmed by 0.040in, a 290-degree duration cam, and a nice fat six-into-two-into-one exhaust manifold leading

Ron Lambrecht's Spit 6 features the original GT6 bulge, with another one added to clear the SU carbs. It's possibly larger than strictly necessary, and skilfully constructed in steel.

The car has a purposeful stance, with a little negative camber on the rear. The suspension has plenty of optional adjustment.

This Spit 6 is considerably faster than a GT6, with something like 120+bhp available due to Ron's tweaks; the GT6 roof and most of the glasshouse have been removed.

to a Monza twin exhaust – although Kas Kastner says a free-flow twin exhaust drops 6bhp, so it might not be a bad idea for Ron to discreetly block off one of the tail-pipes. The Triumph six can't fail to make a delicious noise anyway, irrespective of the exhaust system. There's a TR6 intake manifold with two HS6 SU carbs. Distributor is TR6, with Tectronic ignition, and there is an external oil cooler, an electric fan on the standard GT6 radiator, and an electric fuel pump. The flywheel is lightened, and the GT6 all-synchro gearbox is standard, with quite a low 3.63:1 diff and no overdrive or fifth gear.

The design of the engine mods is for power at high revs,

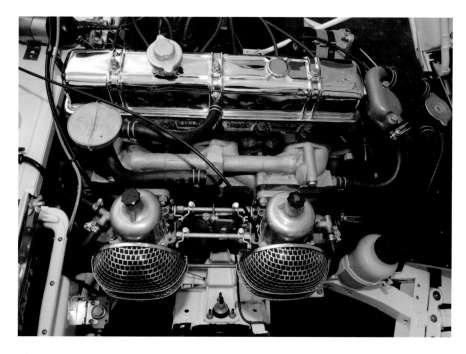

SUs rather than Strombergs have been fitted, with a manifold originally intended for a TR6. There are more tuning parts available for SU carbs than for Strombergs.

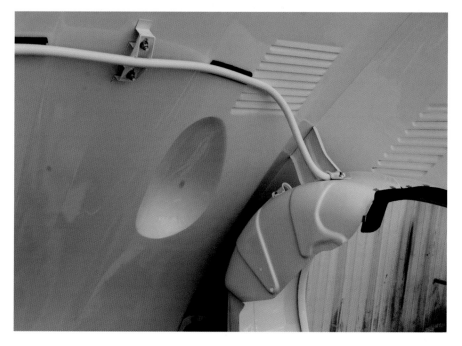

The extra bulge for the SU air filters has been beautifully executed: you literally can't see the join. The rest of the GT6 bonnet is standard, and its 1970 date matches the Spitfire body.

The view down the bonnet along a San Diego highway looks fairly tempting, and is matched by the musical howl of the Triumph straight six.

so the main idea is that the car should go flat out in terms of acceleration, which it definitely does. Ron isn't bothered that at highway cruising speeds the engine is revving rather high and is fairly noisy. It's more or less on cam at highways speeds, so there is instant power available with just a dab on the throttle.

In order to improve the handling to deal with the extra performance, Ron has sharpened up the suspension with polybushes throughout and Spax adjustable shocks all round. The rear shock mounts have been modified to move the pivot point further out and to provide longer travel. The Rotoflex couplings have been retained. There is a stiff ⁷/₈in diameter anti-roll bar at the front. The GT6 brakes are bigger than the Spitfire brakes, and Ron has cross-drilled the discs for additional cooling.

One major improvement to the performance is the roll-over bar. The reassurance of only suffering very unpleasant results from a roll-over, rather than anything horrific or terminal, encourages you to take a much more robust approach to driving, which dramatically improves the performance of any car. I never do anything really silly without a roll-over bar, and once cheerfully agreed when I was accused of cowardice when I refused to go out on

Llandow circuit in a Lada fitted with a Rover V8 and no rollcage. I have, however, thoroughly enjoyed Z-Cars boss Chris Allanson's full-on 100mph++ (160km/h++) frighten-the-journo demonstration ride in a fully caged rear-mid-Honda-engined Z-Cars Mini, despite the bruising, and the keeping of hands in pockets because there's no window mat and you need to keep everything you value inside the car in case it gets into a proper bouncy barrel-roll. So yes, we like roll-over bars.

Ron didn't really do any scary driving on our little demo cruise, but the car definitely felt eager, planted and generally well sorted. The ride was civilized, and there's a lot to be said for Colin Chapman's formula of soft springs and hard shocks.

OLIVIER MARTINEAU'S SPITFIRE 1500

Olivier's car is precisely what this book is about. Olivier Martineau quietly worked his way through a nice low-mileage 1980 Spitfire until it looked and felt the way he wanted it to. There was no big budget and no big engineering drama, just a series of weekend projects in a logical progression. This is in Vancouver, Canada, and

Olivier Martineau's Spitfire has nice detailing on the front: bumper changes and permanent plastic underbonnet side valance panels, fitted with MGB indicator/sidelights.

the 1980 bumpers fitted to US and Canadian export Spitfires are large and fairly grotesque. Olivier removed them and fitted European spec chrome bumpers and Euro headlights, then used MGB sidelight/indicator units and replaced the inevitably rusty front indicator/valance panels below the bumpers with plastic ones. These take a lot of punishment from grit and salt, and should have been made out of plastic to start with.

The body was in pretty good shape, so Olivier moved smartly on to the suspension. The 1980-spec rear Spitfire suspension was basically all right, so the first step was a set of anti-roll or sway bars back and front. These were made by Addco, who specialize in them. They don't prevent the suspension from working and remaining comfortable, but they do minimize body roll and flatten cornering very usefully. The front bar is 1in in diameter, and the rear $^7/_8$in. The car is fitted with polybushes throughout to add

The 1980 Martineau Spitfire benefits from significant visual improvements over the standard ugly spec US bumpers, and the 15in wheels do it no visual harm either.

Giovanni Michelotti contributed a great deal to the Triumph marque over his years of designing for them. Karmann's redesign of the back end was sympathetic and skilful.

Fat back wheels and tyres update the look of the Spitfire, and up to a point, improve grip. The contact patch between tyre and road still has to be properly loaded, though.

more precision to the suspension movements, and the shocks are PRO adjustables all round. Spring rates remain standard.

The brakes are significantly uprated, with braided lines, PRO vented discs and Wilwood four-pot calipers.

Wheel diameter has gone up from 13in to 15in with a set of Konig alloys in the Minilite style, which required some rolling of the inner front wheel arches. These wheels make the car look and feel more modern and more purposeful, and the extra rubber is not excessive. Lightweight alloy wheels also reduce unsprung weight, which is always a bonus.

With the car more than ready to handle more performance, Olivier got going on the engine. It remains the original 1500, and releasing it from the strangulation of a single smogged Stromberg and exhaust gas recirculation gear by fitting a pair of fat HS4 SU carbs added a significant percentage to the bhp – from about 50bhp, Olivier guesses it's now about 75bhp. The air filters are K&N, and the needles and springs in the carb have been chosen by trial and error for the best results. Ignition is Pertronix, and the slightly hotter plugs are fed by fat ND silicone plug leads. This is all good thinking – almost any engine, high performance or not, will run much better if the little details are accurate and kept serviced and fresh. The exhaust manifold is a 2in mandrel-bent, stainless steel, four-into-one running into a Borla silencer.

The 1500cc engine is less than enthusiastic about revving, so Olivier combined an overdrive diff ratio with a Ford Type 9 gearbox swap, giving him a useful cruising gear. The torque of the engine won't have been compromised by any of his tuning moves, so there is enough

power to get up reasonable hills with just a judicious squeeze of the throttle.

By making sensible choices and picking away at the project at a leisurely pace, Olivier has made the very most of his Spitfire without committing any really serious time or money to it.

BILL JACKSON'S GT6

Bill Jackson's lightly tweaked but quite original GT6 has the most dramatic back story. Bill has been involved with the car since 1970, when his San Diego repair shop did some work on it for the owner, who never came back to collect it. He put a mechanic's lien on the car, took ownership of it and tried to sell it. It kept coming back. At one point he got a very sad surprise when the original owner's widow asked if he still had the Triumph: it turned out that the reason the original owner hadn't come back for his car was that he had been killed in Vietnam. Bill gave the widow the Blue Book value for the car, which at that point had been temporarily sold on.

Five times Bill tried to get rid of the GT6, but everybody who bought it and drove it away brought it back after a while.

The final time Bill sold it, in 1986, he thought it was going to stay sold, but another mechanic had fitted the wire wheel hubs the wrong way round, and a wheel unwound itself and fell off. This was on a highway, and the errant wheel bounced into the windscreen of an oncoming Buick. The Triumph's owner left the scene of the accident. Bill was woken up by the police at 4am, and arrested for a hit and run as he was still registered as the owner.

Bill Jackson's GT6 is still in sound and original condition – the San Diego climate is very kind to the metalwork of old British cars, although it's less gentle on the paint and upholstery.

Blue California plate has been with the car since it was new. Other than slightly mismatched paint on the hatchback after the fitting of new screen rubbers, the paint is original.

Rotoflex couplings have been replaced by constant velocity joints, an entirely better idea, particularly as high quality Rotoflex rubbers are not available as of mid-2015.

His wife at this point said, 'Okay, this is silly, the car has obviously decided that it wants you to own it and there's nothing you can do about that. You might as well just give in and keep it.' That was in 1987, and Bill has had the Triumph ever since. It now has 107,000 miles (170,000km) of happy driving on it, sometimes on long trips and sometimes as a daily driver. It has never been on a trailer. The body and paint are still mostly original, which is one of the benefits of living in Southern California.

Bill has been quietly improving the car in many small ways ever since 1987. The engine and overdrive have been left alone apart from very regular oil changes, and keeping the weight of the left foot off the clutch pedal has prolonged the life of the crankshaft thrust washers by some 80,000 miles (130,000km). The exhaust aft of the manifold is from a Spitfire.

San Diego summer temperatures can be brutal, but Bill says a four-core radiator and really tight shrouding

Spax adjustable shock absorbers seem to be a popular choice for the smaller Triumphs; seen here in Bill's GT6 with the post-Rotoflex axle specification.

Front suspension in Bill's GT6 consists of Canley Classic hubs and uprights, with balljoints and useful adjustability, combined again with Spax adjustable shocks.

from the main air intake to the radiator gap are enough to keep the engine temperature within bounds. Bill has combined the overdrive gearbox with a 2.73:1 differential ratio to provide cruising at 3,000rpm for 90mph (145km/h), which is quite relaxed, but with the torque from the six, first gear is still not too over-geared for town use.

The suspension has received most of Bill's attention. At the front he has used Canley Classics front hubs and vertical links, with ball joints top and bottom, adjustable at the end of the wishbones to the zero degrees of camber he favours. Shocks are two-way-adjustable Spaxes. The front brake discs are drilled and he used

braided lines throughout, and there is a 1¼in anti-roll bar at the front.

At the back, he experimented with a rear coil spring set-up, but didn't like the fact that the mountings were on a thin and unbraced part of the bodywork and not on the chassis. If the set-up had been adapted to attach the shock mount to the chassis, the angle of the shock absorber would have affected its leverage angle to the point where it wouldn't have worked properly. The coil-over-shock approach could have been made to work with welded braced mounts on the body, but Bill just went back to the transverse spring.

The rear suspension is about to get a major change, with a Canley aluminium rear hub and axles with CV joints to replace the Rotoflex couplings. Bill says the Rotoflexes are now only manufactured in China and their life is now even shorter than the originals – so it's time to upgrade to a conceptually better system. Of course CV joints wear as well, but not at the same speed.

Inside, Bill has been happy to leave the stock interior virtually as it came, with two exceptions: he upgraded the seats to late-model TR6, which has made long trips much more comfortable; and he insulated the floors, which has made a big difference to interior noise levels.

MAX MCMILLAN'S GT8

Max McMillan's outrageous GT6 is fitted with a 5000cc Ford V8. This is going to be fun, I thought, when I drove it for a story in *Triumph World*. I expected it to be a monster, but remarkably, it turned out to be primarily a pleasant cruiser, with better manners than a standard GT6. I didn't expect this from a 5-litre V8 car built on a fairly standard Herald-based ladder chassis. I've driven and written about MGBs with American V8 conversions, and they can successfully be both tyre-shredding monsters and civilized tourers, depending purely on throttle foot pressure. This is because the designers made the MGB a monocoque, but then added back in quite a lot of chassis as well, so an MGB GT is a very solid object indeed – particularly before it rusts again. I didn't think the Triumph's less solidly connected body and chassis would respond well to massive torque, but I was wrong.

The first surprise was that the small-block Ford V8 is a much better and more suitable engine for the car than the standard straight six. What? Well, with alloy heads it weighs around 40lb (18kg) less than the original Triumph engine. It is also only four cylinders long, and that puts the weight behind the front axle. Both of those factors are unarguably

Max McMillan's GT6 is now a GT8, with a 5-litre Ford 302 V8. Astonishingly, the Ford V8 weighs less than the original Triumph six when fitted with aluminium heads.

significant dynamic improvements. The engine in question was a 302cu in (5-litre) Mustang-type V8. It uses a 'thinwall' casting process, and this particular engine was fitted with a pair of aluminium high-performance cylinder heads.

The aluminium heads, although used in this case mostly to cut weight, are performance parts and have big valves and improved porting. The uprated pistons were matched to the heads for more compression, the cam is slightly aggressive but the engine still idles well, and the Edelbrock carb is capable of flowing 700cu ft per minute at full chat through the Edelbrock intake manifold, compared to something like 260cfm from the Strombergs. The cam is mildly rude but still what North Americans call 'streetable'. There are fabricated tubular exhaust manifolds

wandering through the chassis rails to a set of budget JEGS sidepipes. There's a custom oversize copper radiator with shrouding and electric fan: obviously the original radiator wasn't up to the job. A conservative estimate of the available power is around 300bhp with 340lb ft of torque. 300bhp is not extreme for a 302cu in V8, and of course you only use 30bhp to drive to work.

Fitting a Ford V8 without a matching uprated transmission and chassis isn't really an option, though – for example, if you fitted a V8 to a standard Triumph transmission and dropped the clutch, you could take bets as to whether the teeth in the gearbox or those in the diff would strip first.

The reason for this conversion was that the original engine had blown up, and it was far easier and cheaper

Once you know about the weight and the aft repositioning of the short, fat engine it's not a surprise to find that the car drives and handles a good bit better than the original GT6, whether cruising or bruising.

to fit a local secondhand V8 than to have a new or rebuilt Triumph engine shipped 5,000 miles (8,000km). This particular V8 happened to come with a four-speed Toploader gearbox from the 1960s, but nearly all manual Mustangs since the 1970s come with the excellent five-speed T5 gearbox. Having sorted the gearbox, the Triumph diff would have been the next part to explode, but the owner's dad happened to have a dead XJ6, which was raided for its diff and axles. That was top luck, because the Jag diff is a Salisbury and will take whatever abuse you care to hurl at it.

You might think that the torsional stresses from three times the original power would have consequences for the bodyshell, even with the bracing that Max added, but ten years of hard use without a single stress fracture suggests otherwise. There is heavy tubular bracing connecting the front of the chassis to the bulkhead, which also carries brackets for coil-over front shocks, and there is a simple, sturdy framework at the back that mounts the diff. Shortened rear Jag top wishbones work with weight-bearing driveshafts in the Jag independent format.

A brake balancing valve is required, as the back brakes are bigger than the fronts, but other than that, the building of this car could have been carried out by most people who have read this far. There is MIG welding, most of which could be fairly agricultural in nature, and the only thing you would need help with is the bending of tubing for the chassis braces and the manifolds. The chassis bracing might in any case be better in the form of lighter space-framing, rather than the two big bars.

The V8 sits quite comfortably in the engine bay. The original chassis is retained, although considerably beefed up with extra tubing welded to the chassis and the front bulkhead.

The very reasonable fuel economy achievable from a mildly tuned, manual American V8 cruising at 1,500rpm in a light and aerodynamic car might come as a surprise, too: Max hasn't calculated the mpg, because it hasn't been an issue. I once had a Cobra replica with an even larger 350 Chevy V8 in it with an autobox and the same Jag rear end, and that got 20mpg when ambling.

WILLIE PLATT'S T6 LE MANS

Willie Platt's T6 Le Mans was bought as a mostly complete project, with some interesting ideas applied. Under the bonnet of a replica of a historic Triumph racing car, probably the last thing you would ever expect to find is an MG engine, but that is exactly what is in the engine bay. Dynamically, this is far from a bad idea. The engine is a clever, lightweight, powerful K-series 1.8-litre dohc 4-cylinder with an advanced variable-valve control system

Inboard of the chassis bracing tube, the fat exhaust manifold pipes snake around the chassis and the starter. The pipes could have been hidden under the car, but Max likes sidepipe thunder. I don't, as you really only hear one side.

Even with the bulge, the bonnet won't clear the large single four-barrel carb and air filter, so an extra scoop/bulge had to be added. The new frame retains the bonnet's stiffness.

The original Triumph diff would have given up the ghost fairly quickly, so an entire Jaguar XJ6 rear end has been transplanted in. These are unbreakable, although over-braked for a Triumph.

(VVC) that achieves a very flat torque curve, ideal for a light and agile car that might be twitchy if the power delivery were at all lumpy. It runs an MGF throttle body and a MEMS ECU. There's a precedent, of course: the 1500 Spitfire engine is also the 1500 MG Midget engine. The gearbox is a Ford Type 9 five-speed, and the final drive ratio is a low 3.63, so there will be fearsome acceleration available in the lower gears.

The 13in alloy Dolomite wheels are an interesting choice, and they keep the faith with Triumph. However, the choices made demonstrate vividly that when it comes to playing with your own car, you can do whatever you

The T6 is a replica of the Le Mans racing Spitfires of the 1960s. It is also an excellent way of replacing and uprating a damaged or rusted-out bodyshell.

The engine may be shiny and modern, but the suspension on this T6 is visibly pure Spitfire, with a coat of paint and possibly an uprated set of shock absorbers.

The T6 bodyshell and bonnet are an accurate recreation of the Le Mans Spits, but the engine fitted to this example is actually a modern K-series MG engine, anachronistic but rapid.

like, and if assorted figures from the history of Triumph and MG are spinning in their graves, that would be their business.

The body and bonnet are fibreglass replicas of the Le Mans Spitfires, and the construction of the car is more or less the same as a normal Spitfire restoration. You remove the bonnet and then the body tub, and restore the chassis. If it's an ordinary Spitfire, you weld on new sills and floors, patch repair the bonnet, paint it all and bolt it back on, and trim it. If it's a Le Mans replica, you save a year or two. Skip the resto, just bolt the GRP body tub and bonnet on, paint it and trim it (*see* www.triumphspitfire lemans.com).

THE AUTHOR'S MIDGE

We're getting well outside the remit of everyday modifications, but if you're still at the stage of pondering a Triumph rather than trying to improve one, I recommend taking a look at the options within the world of Triumph-based kit cars. These can be remarkably cheap and can offer a lot of fun, both in terms of pottering about changing things or just going a little faster – the power-to-weight ratio is the key to performance, not just power. A Triumph Herald 13/60 with 60bhp, shorn of a third of its weight, is thereby 30 per cent faster. If Lotus's Colin Chapman were still around, you could ask him about the concept of adding lightness: his cars always went quite quickly, albeit not necessarily always for very long.

The author in his freshly built, Vitesse-based Midge, in about 1980. This picture was taken close to the single Ealing lock-up garage in which it was built.

My own Triumph kit car is a Midge, a design by Brit John Cowperthwaite. It was intended to be based on a Triumph Herald chassis and mechanicals. It's clever: you buy a sheet of paper with full-size plans marked on it, and glue the plans down on to thick sheets of ¾in plywood. Then you cut them into a jigsaw with a jig saw, assemble, glue and bolt it together as a 1930s-style body, skin it with thin aluminium and attach it to your Herald chassis. The kit is still available now through the Midge Owners' and Builders' Club. More details are in the bodywork and interior chapter (Chapter 8).

My own example was the first 6-cylinder Midge, built out of the wreckage of a Vitesse that my late mother crashed. It was turned into a Midge and given back to her, and she continued driving it into her eighties. There is just about enough room to squeeze the six in, using the short back and long front body design options, and of course a 6-cylinder Midge goes like greased lightning. Maybe 105bhp with my ported head, low gearing and

After many years, the Midge now lives in a garden in Yorkshire, looking a little tatty but still very much intact: kit-grade chassis steel and marine plywood last for a very long time.

The Triumph 2-litre straight six was jammed into the space designed for a Herald engine. It looks as though I was changing the plugs in this photo. Engine access is bliss in all small Triumphs, including this one.

weighing probably around 1,100lb (500kg), it will take out lesser 911s and has taken particular pleasure in seeing off E-Types, at least to the other side of the traffic lights. Which is, after all, what counts.

Other than a couple of gearbox rebuilds, one over-drive overhaul and some porting and head work, the only change from the original Vitesse mechanicals has been the abandonment of the entire Rotoflex independent Vitesse rear suspension, and its replacement by a Triumph Dolomite live rear axle. This was mounted on coil-over shocks and located by two triangular-shaped fabricated trailing arms with bushed mounts at the top and bottom of the axle, and single mountings on the chassis. The axle is laterally stabilized by a Panhard rod. It resulted in no further axle problems of any sort, and allowed the wire-wheel hubs to be transferred straight over to the Dolomite axle, which has the same wheel-stud spacing or pitch circle diameter. The Midge has a replacement Triumph-inspired steel chassis to kit-car thickness, and remains rust free after thirty-two years. The marine ply body is also still sound. Both of those aspects of kit cars are worth thinking about, unless you actively enjoy welding car bodywork as a hobby.

The car was inspected and properly registered as a Triumph Midge with a new chassis, retaining its original registration plate. With a new chassis it's not so easy nowadays.

The Vitesse instruments, column and switchgear were transferred to the new dashboard, which was designed with a three-dimensional feature in the middle rather than just being the usual kit-car plank.

index

RELATED TITLES FROM CROWOOD

Everyday Modifications for Your MGB, GT and GTV8
ROGER PARKER
ISBN 978 1 84797 810 3
208pp, 360 illustrations

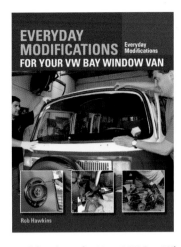

Everyday Modifications for Your VW Bay Window Van
ROB HAWKINS
ISBN 978 1 84797 913 1
192pp, 730 illustrations

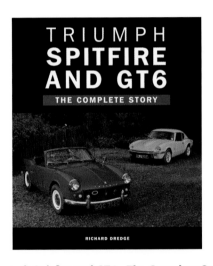

Triumph Spitfire and GT6 – The Complete Story
RICHARD DREDGE
ISBN 978 1 84797 703 8
176pp, 290 illustrations

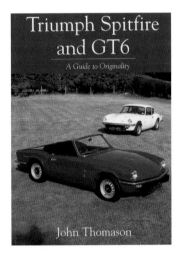

Triumph Spitfire and GT6 – A Guide to Originality
JOHN THOMASON
ISBN 978 1 86126 861 7
160pp, 520 illustrations

In case of difficulty ordering, please contact the Sales Office:
The Crowood Press
Ramsbury
Wiltshire
SN8 2HR
UK
Tel: 44 (0) 1672 520320

enquiries@crowood.com
www.crowood.com